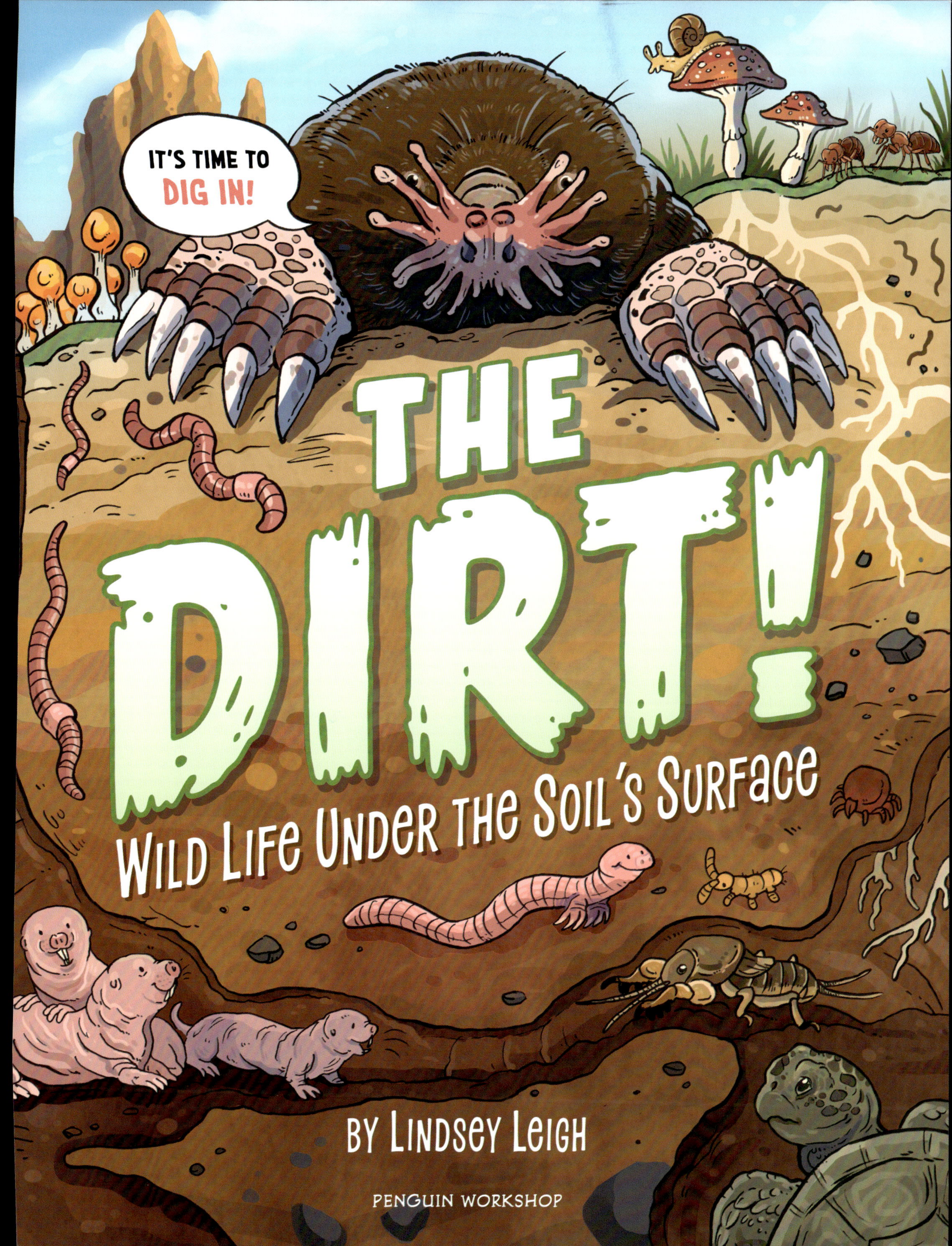
IT'S TIME TO DIG IN!
THE DIRT!
WILD LIFE UNDER THE SOIL'S SURFACE
BY LINDSEY LEIGH
PENGUIN WORKSHOP

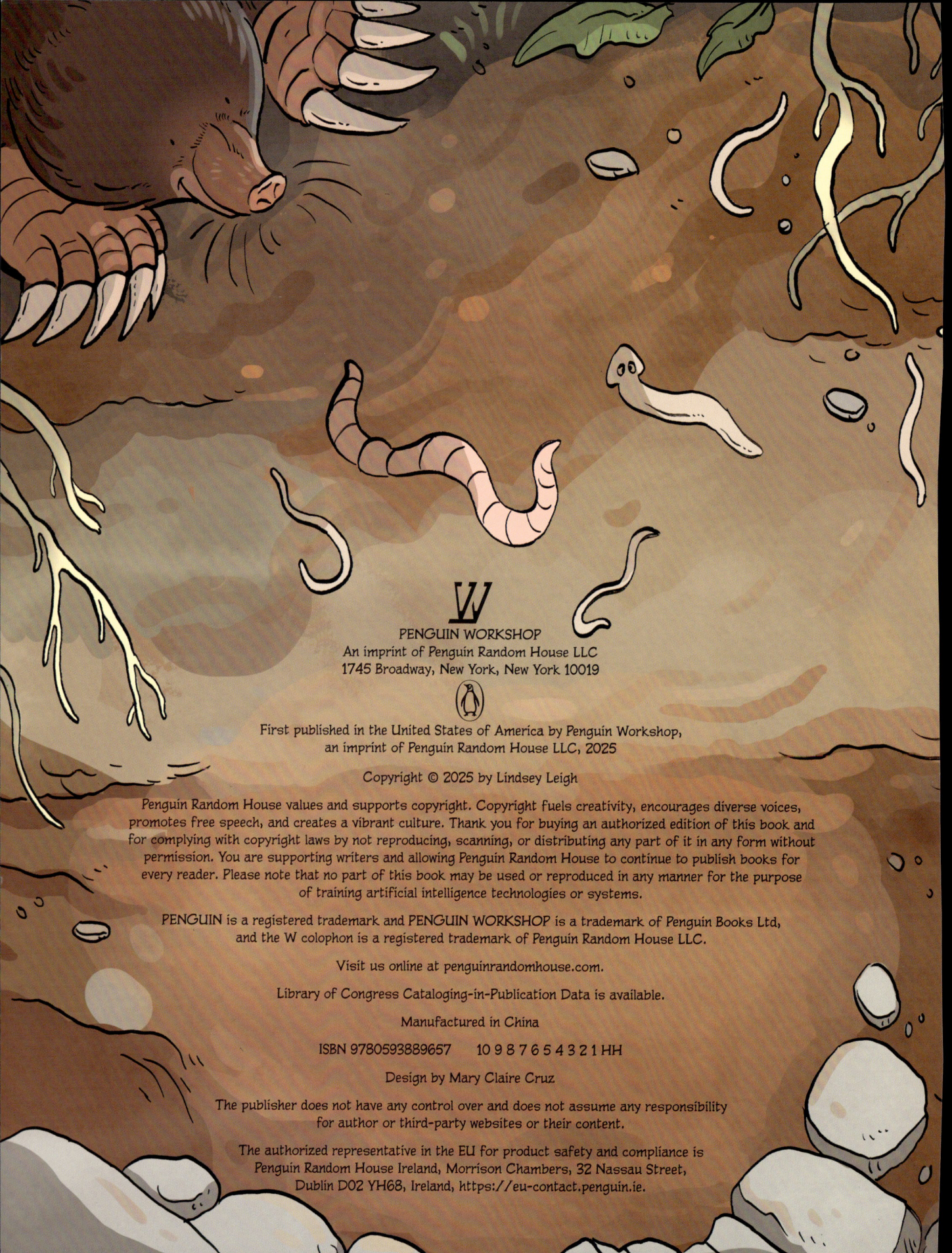

PENGUIN WORKSHOP
An imprint of Penguin Random House LLC
1745 Broadway, New York, New York 10019

First published in the United States of America by Penguin Workshop,
an imprint of Penguin Random House LLC, 2025

Visit us online at penguinrandomhouse.com.

Library of Congress Cataloging-in-Publication Data is available.

Manufactured in China

ISBN 9780593889657   10 9 8 7 6 5 4 3 2 1 HH

Design by Mary Claire Cruz

The publisher does not have any control over and does not assume any responsibility
for author or third-party websites or their content.

The authorized representative in the EU for product safety and compliance is
Penguin Random House Ireland, Morrison Chambers, 32 Nassau Street,
Dublin D02 YH68, Ireland, https://eu-contact.penguin.ie.

CONTENTS

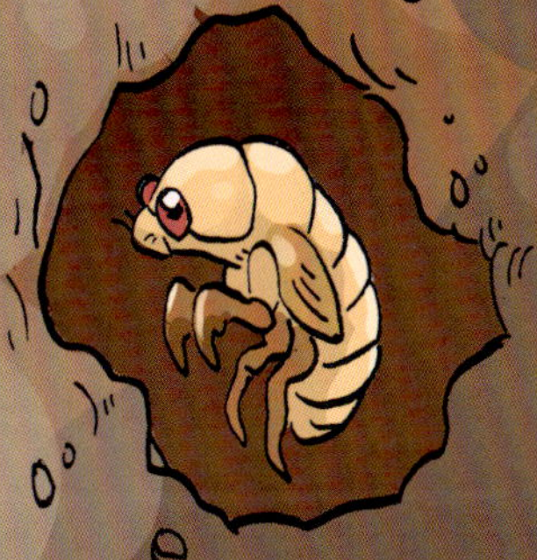

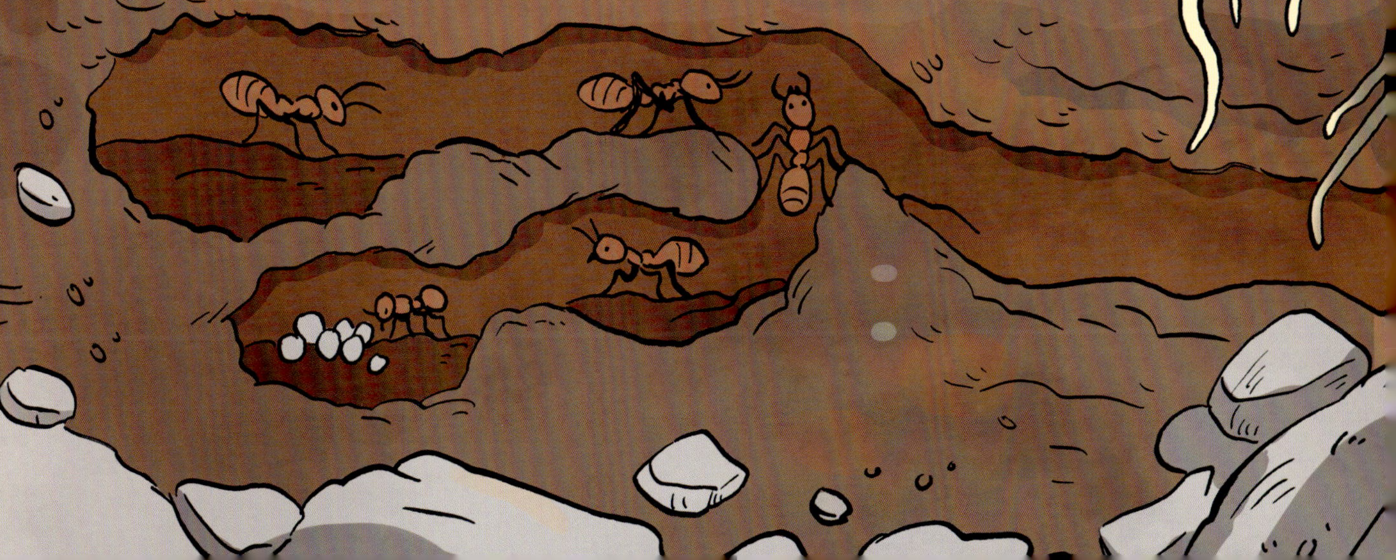

Welcome to the Alien World of THE DIRT!

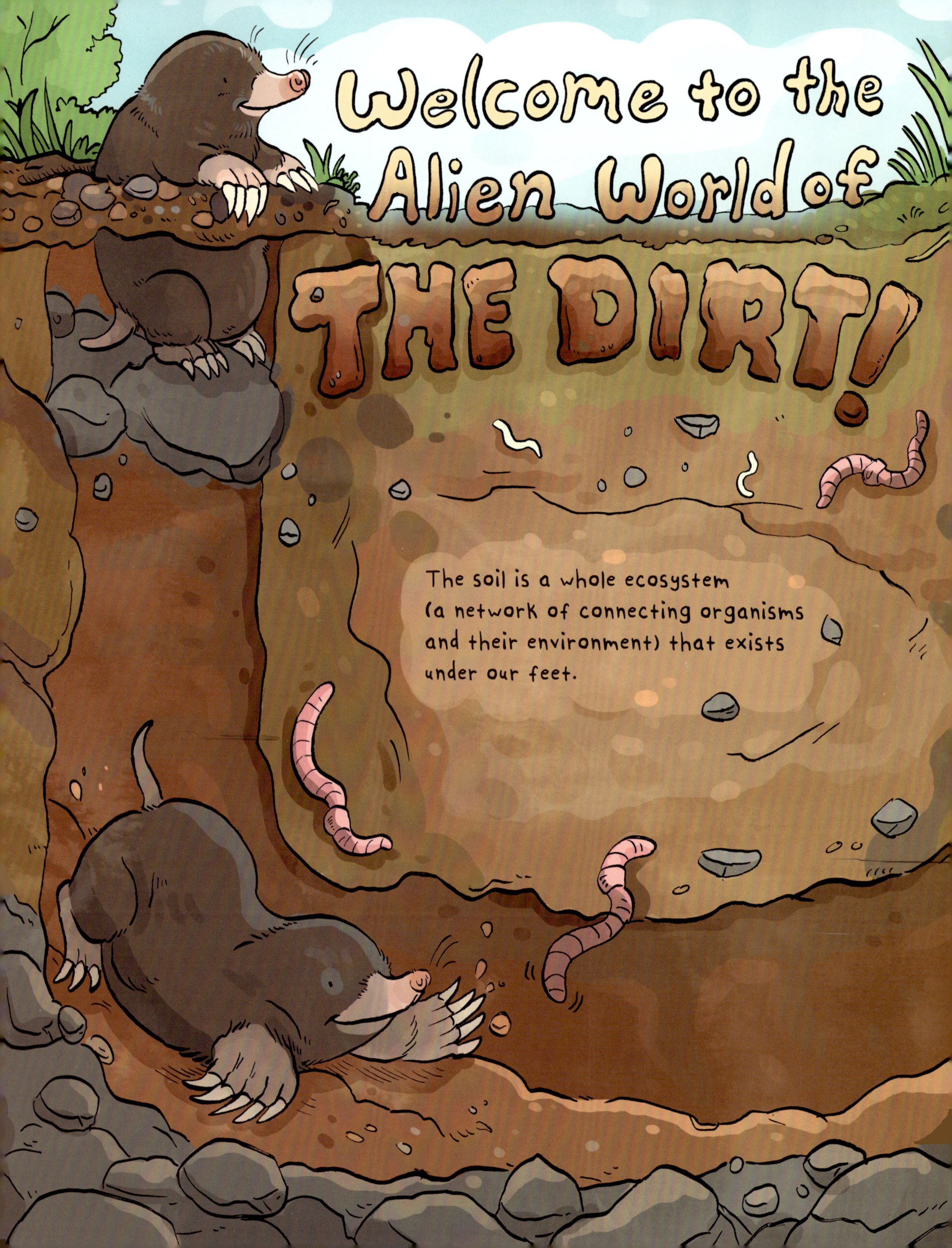

The soil is a whole ecosystem (a network of connecting organisms and their environment) that exists under our feet.

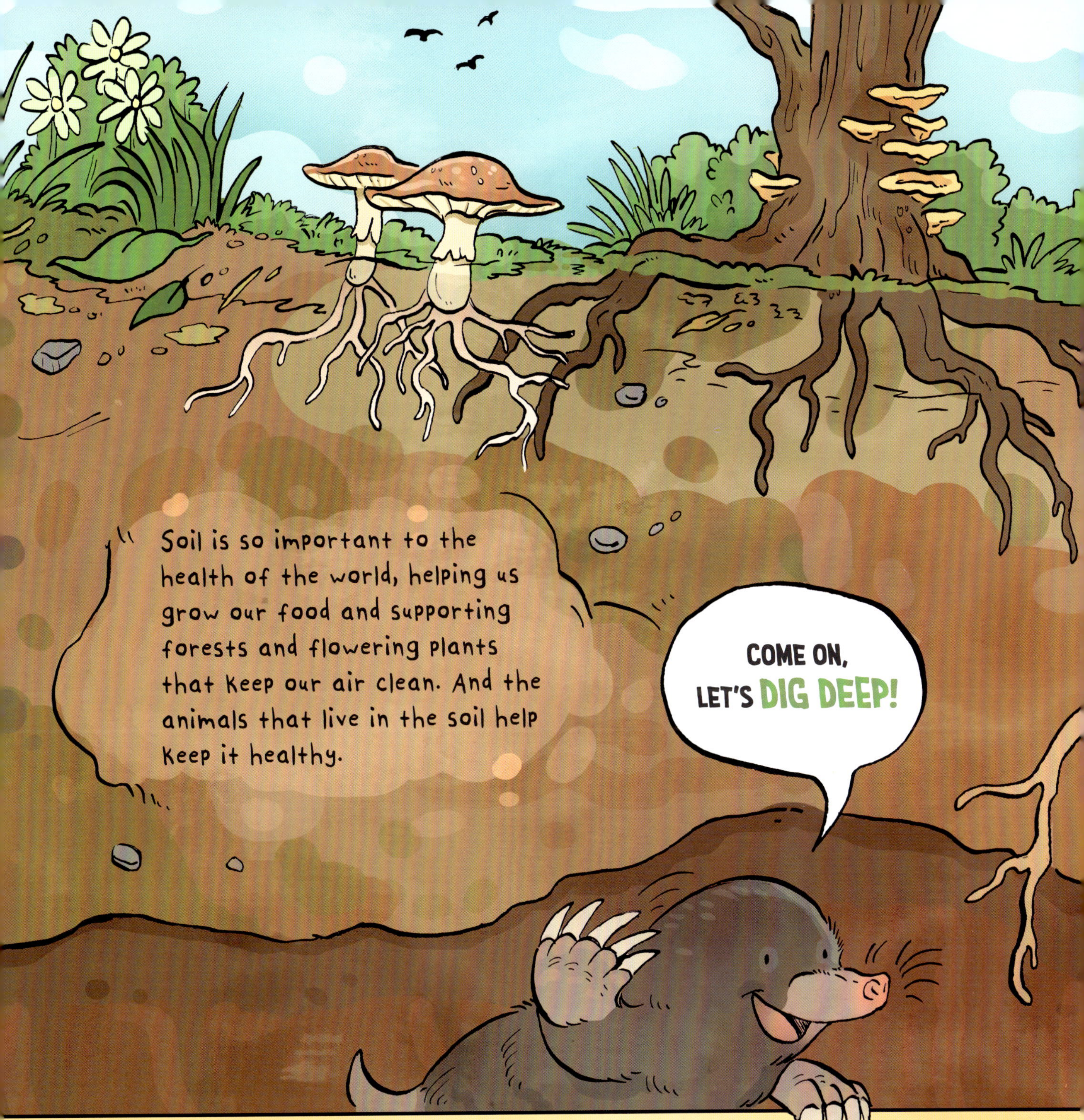
Soil is so important to the health of the world, helping us grow our food and supporting forests and flowering plants that keep our air clean. And the animals that live in the soil help keep it healthy.
COME ON, LET'S DIG DEEP!

DIRT AND SOIL, WHAT'S THE DIFFERENCE?

Dirt alone is lifeless, but soil is healthy and teeming with life. Technically, soil is dirt with added organic matter like dead leaves, dead animals, and poop in it to help plants grow. (*The Dirt!* was just a catchier title!)

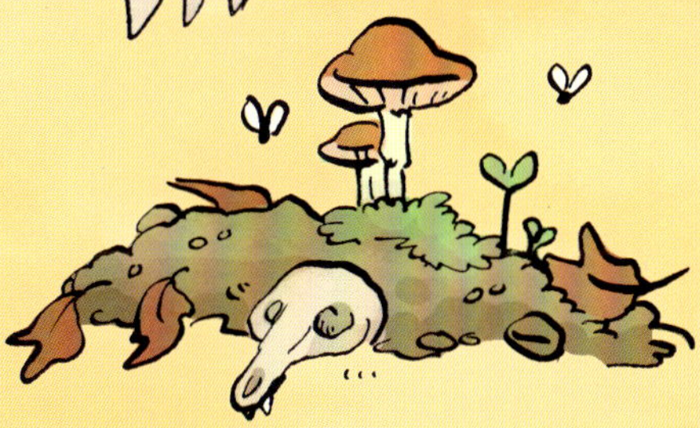

All About the SOIL

This might look like a lifeless hunk of dirt, but a handful of soil is chock-full of life. This handful can contain millions of microbes (tiny organisms that can be seen only with a microscope, such as bacteria).

This small amount of soil can contain more microbes than there are people on the planet! These tiny but mighty organisms are what make the whole soil environment go round. The more life-forms the soil contains, the healthier it will be.

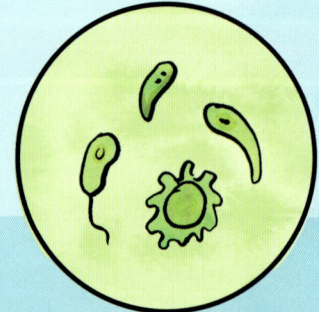

Microfauna
Less than 0.004 inches long

Mesofauna
0.004–0.08 inches

Macrofauna
0.08–1 inch

Megafauna
Larger than an inch

Tiny bacteria and other microscopic organisms are known as microfauna, larger animals are mesofauna, even larger animals are macrofauna, and large burrowing animals like moles are known as megafauna. This book will introduce you to all of them according to size.

Soil is only the thin top layer of earth that covers the surface of the planet, but it is incredibly important. It wraps around the earth like a layer of skin.

New soil forms when rocks and other materials are broken down by erosion, microbes, plants, fungi (organisms that are neither plants nor animals, including molds, yeasts, and the mushrooms you find on your salad), and other small animals.

SOIL DECOMPOSITION For healthy soil, you need decomposition: breakdown and decay.

Organic matter like leaves, plants, dead animals, and poop break down and provide food to soil-dwelling bacteria. Some scientists call this the poop loop! Animals eat this matter, then poop it out to create a richer soil.

Microbes break down nutrients even further into a form that plants can eat. Fungi are also very important to the soil ecosystem: They decompose leaves, fallen trees, and other plant materials; help plants absorb nutrients; and strengthen the soil.

Soil City Food Web

Welcome to Soil City—a bustling community of animals, plants, and bacteria that all depend on one another to survive. The relationships and transfer of energy between each organism here form a web, called the soil food web.

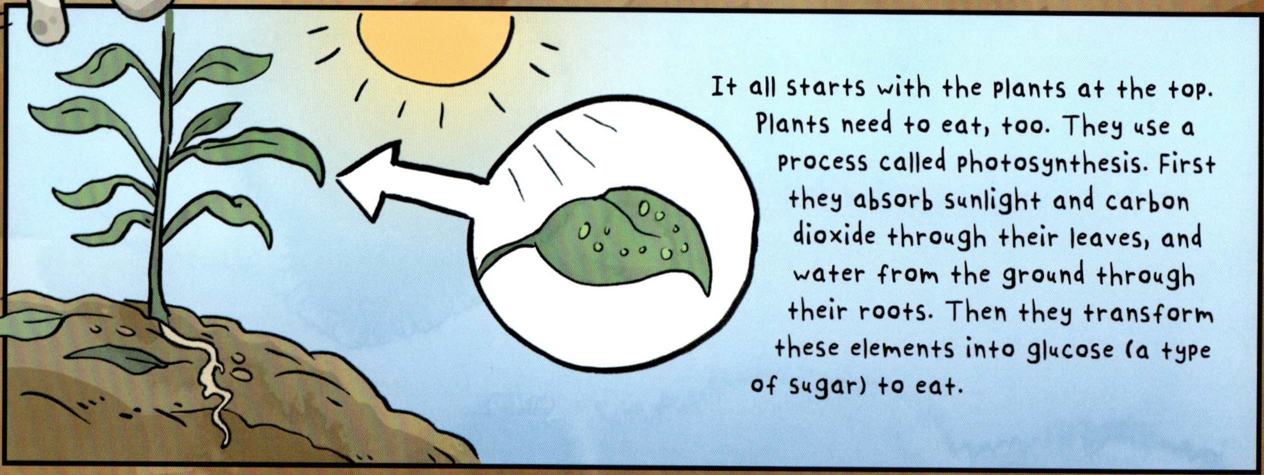
It all starts with the plants at the top. Plants need to eat, too. They use a process called photosynthesis. First they absorb sunlight and carbon dioxide through their leaves, and water from the ground through their roots. Then they transform these elements into glucose (a type of sugar) to eat.

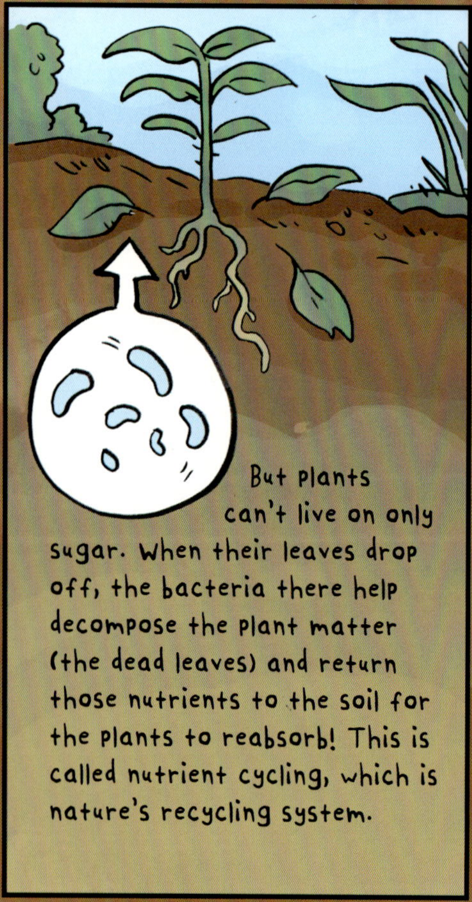
But plants can't live on only sugar. When their leaves drop off, the bacteria there help decompose the plant matter (the dead leaves) and return those nutrients to the soil for the plants to reabsorb! This is called nutrient cycling, which is nature's recycling system.

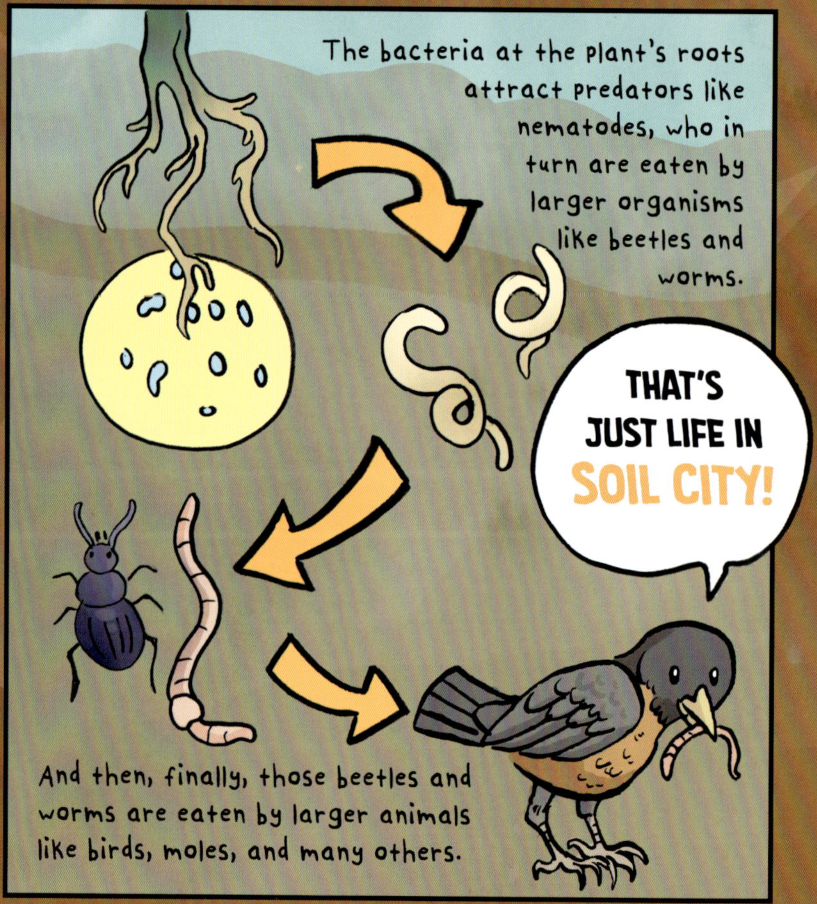
The bacteria at the plant's roots attract predators like nematodes, who in turn are eaten by larger organisms like beetles and worms.
THAT'S JUST LIFE IN SOIL CITY!
And then, finally, those beetles and worms are eaten by larger animals like birds, moles, and many others.

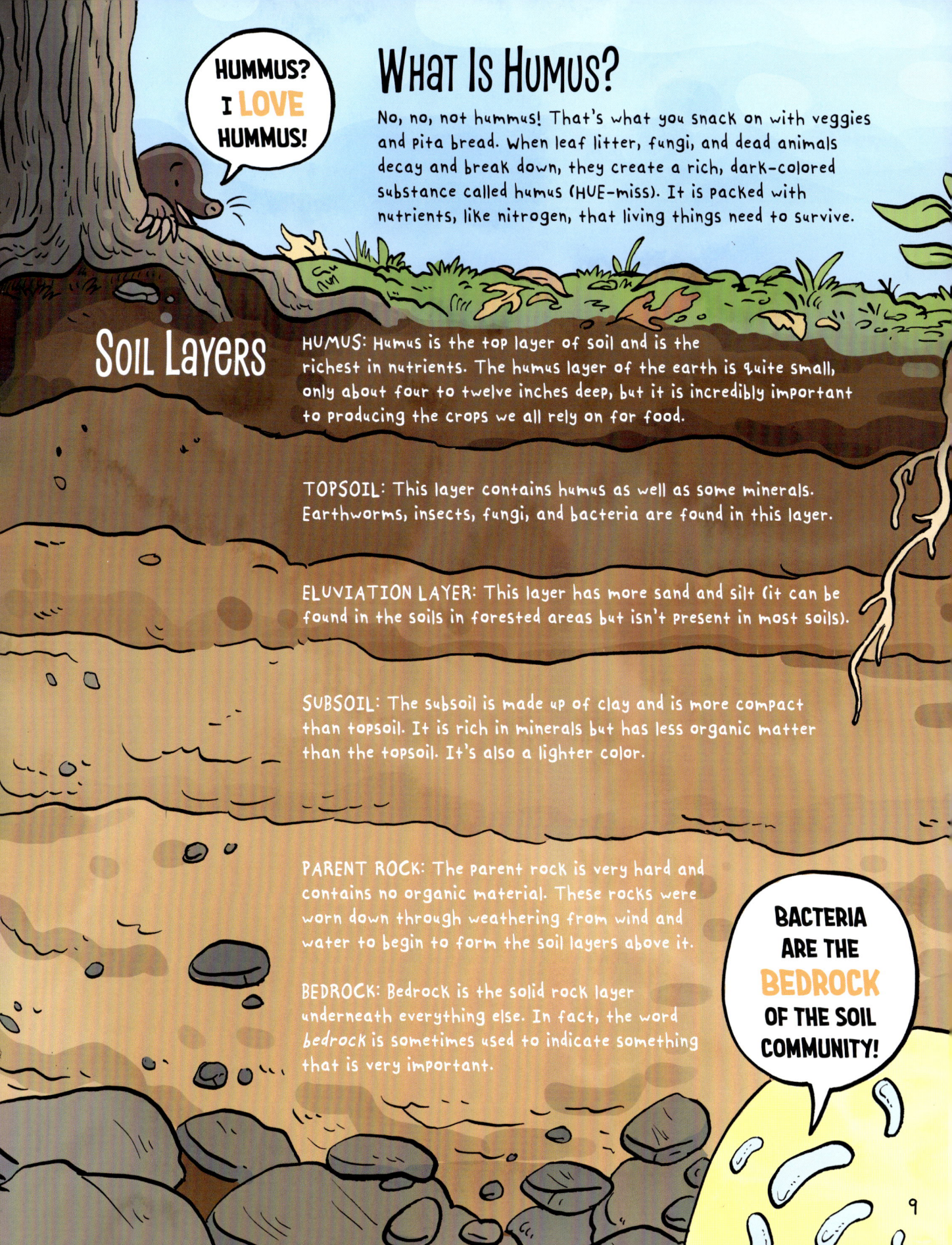

HUMMUS? I LOVE HUMMUS!

What Is Humus?

No, no, not hummus! That's what you snack on with veggies and pita bread. When leaf litter, fungi, and dead animals decay and break down, they create a rich, dark-colored substance called humus (HUE-miss). It is packed with nutrients, like nitrogen, that living things need to survive.

Soil Layers

HUMUS: Humus is the top layer of soil and is the richest in nutrients. The humus layer of the earth is quite small, only about four to twelve inches deep, but it is incredibly important to producing the crops we all rely on for food.

TOPSOIL: This layer contains humus as well as some minerals. Earthworms, insects, fungi, and bacteria are found in this layer.

ELUVIATION LAYER: This layer has more sand and silt (it can be found in the soils in forested areas but isn't present in most soils).

SUBSOIL: The subsoil is made up of clay and is more compact than topsoil. It is rich in minerals but has less organic matter than the topsoil. It's also a lighter color.

PARENT ROCK: The parent rock is very hard and contains no organic material. These rocks were worn down through weathering from wind and water to begin to form the soil layers above it.

BEDROCK: Bedrock is the solid rock layer underneath everything else. In fact, the word *bedrock* is sometimes used to indicate something that is very important.

BACTERIA ARE THE BEDROCK OF THE SOIL COMMUNITY!

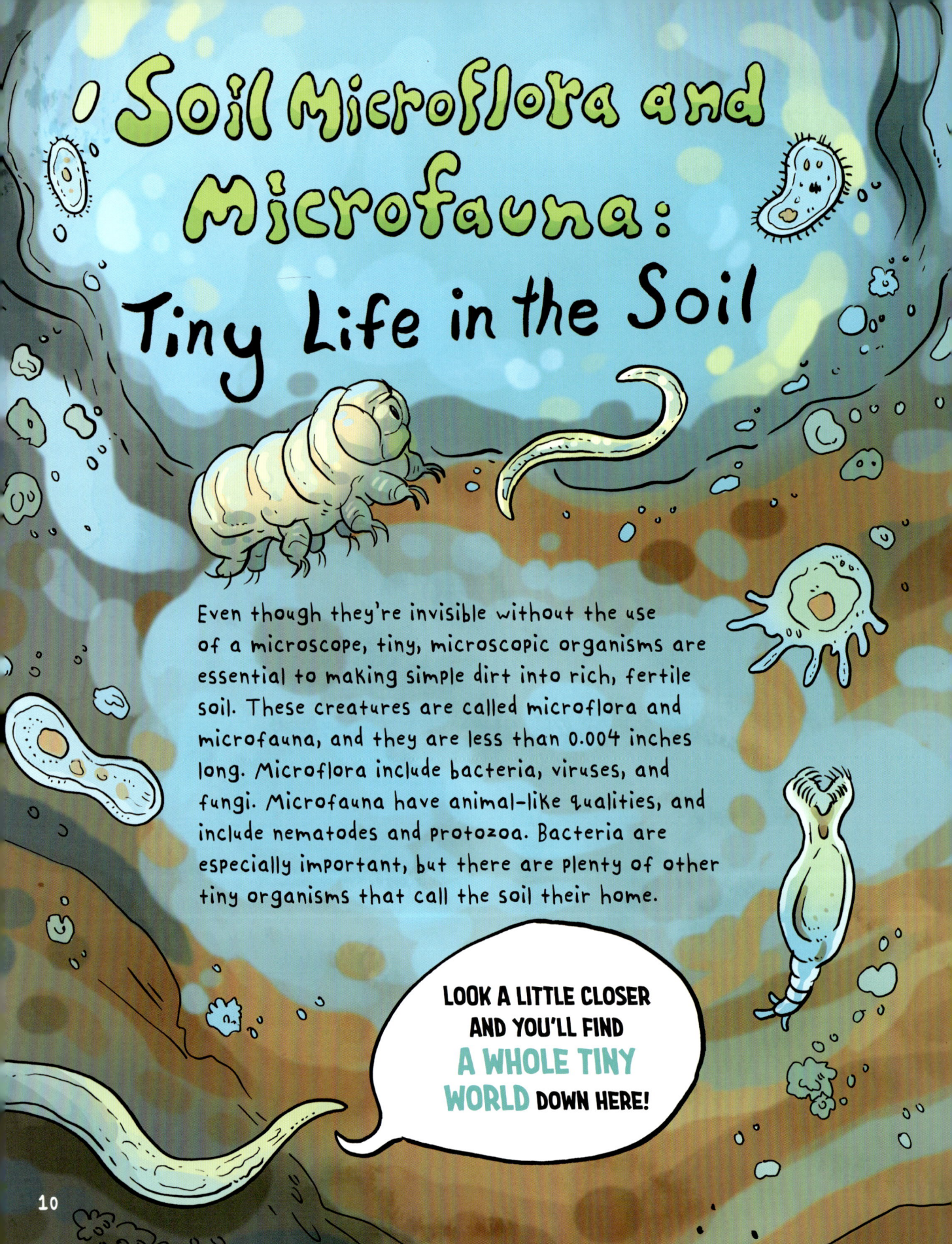

Soil Microflora and Microfauna: Tiny Life in the Soil

Even though they're invisible without the use of a microscope, tiny, microscopic organisms are essential to making simple dirt into rich, fertile soil. These creatures are called microflora and microfauna, and they are less than 0.004 inches long. Microflora include bacteria, viruses, and fungi. Microfauna have animal-like qualities, and include nematodes and protozoa. Bacteria are especially important, but there are plenty of other tiny organisms that call the soil their home.

LOOK A LITTLE CLOSER AND YOU'LL FIND **A WHOLE TINY WORLD** DOWN HERE!

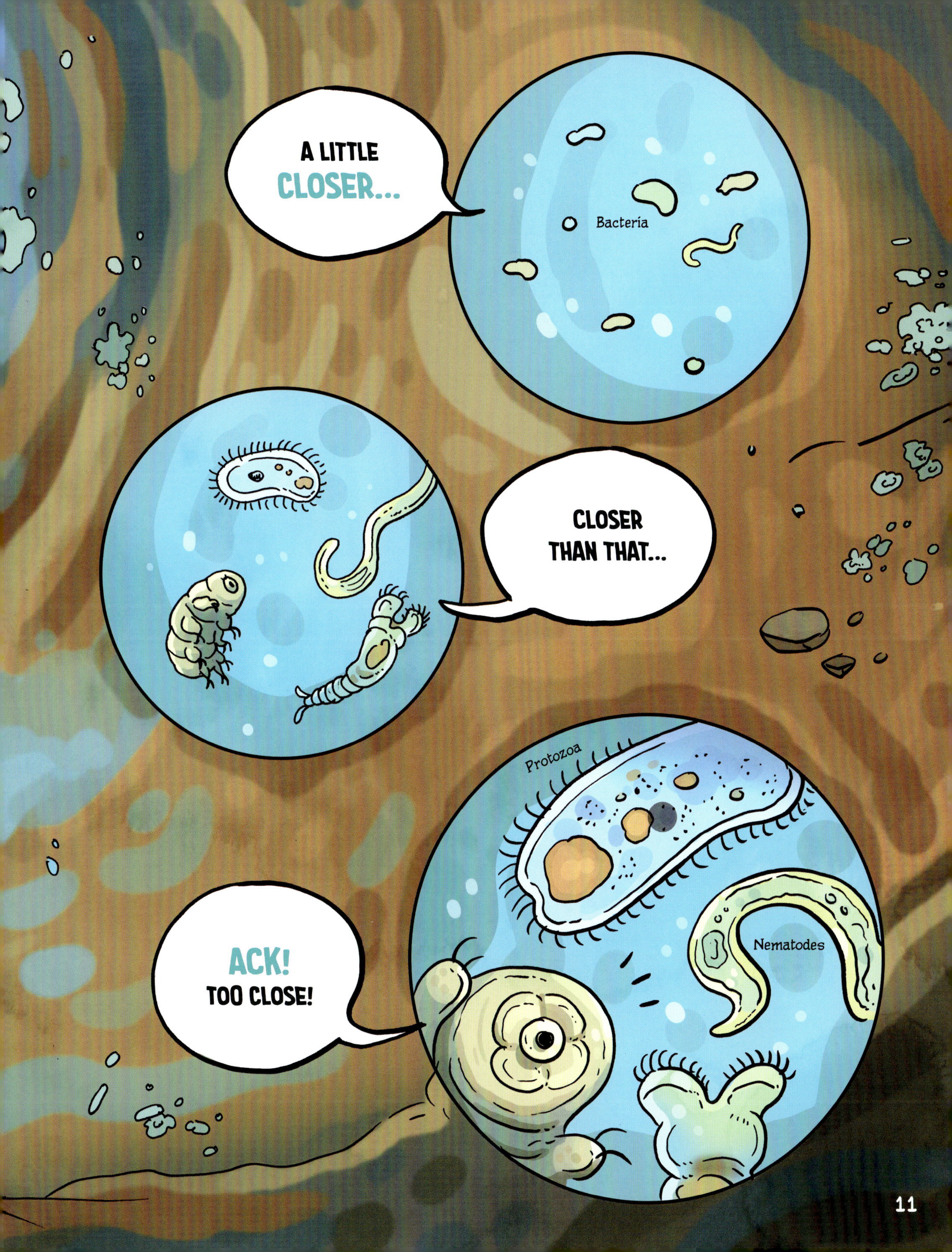
A LITTLE CLOSER...
Bacteria
CLOSER THAN THAT...
Protozoa
Nematodes
ACK! TOO CLOSE!

Brilliant Bacteria

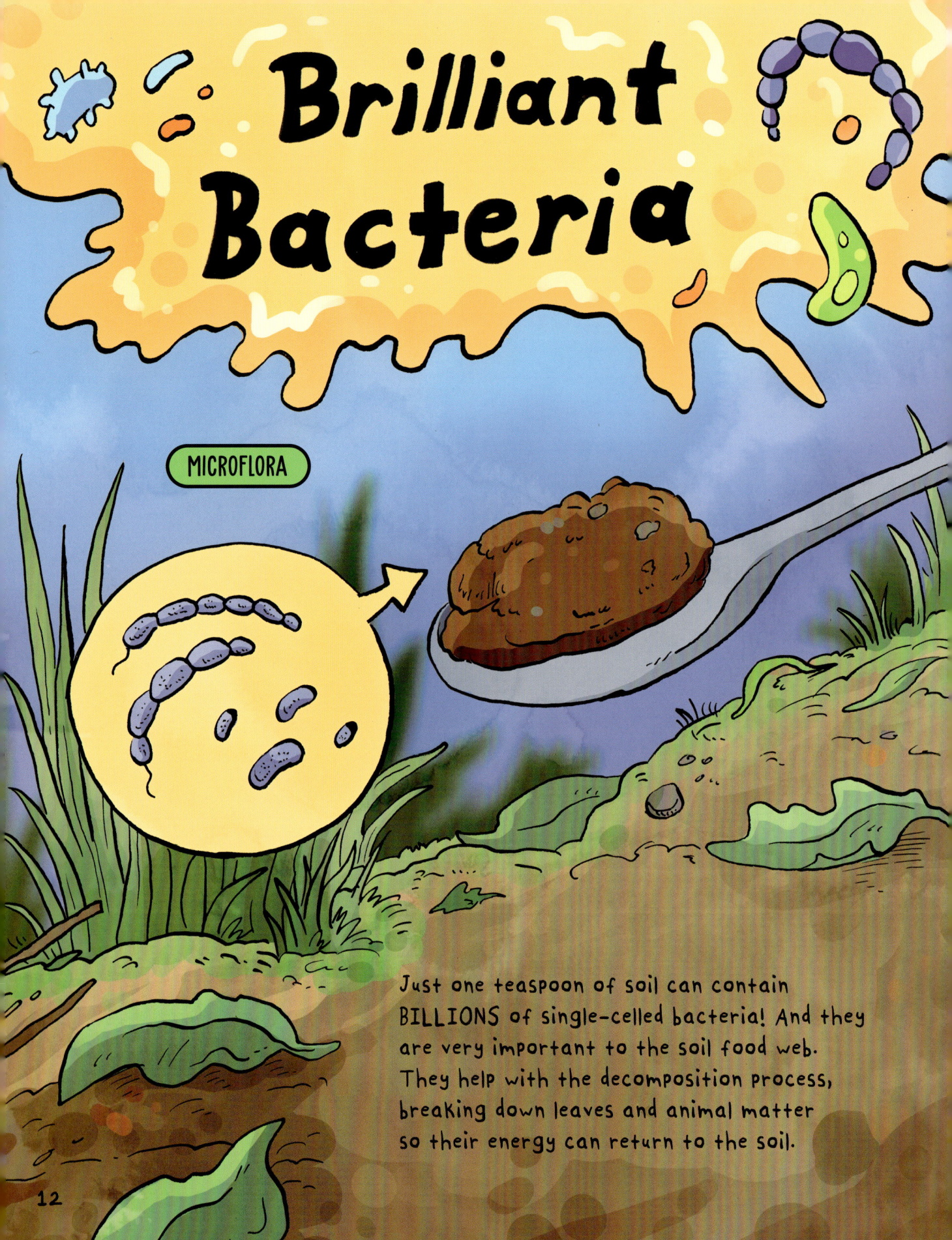

MICROFLORA

Just one teaspoon of soil can contain BILLIONS of single-celled bacteria! And they are very important to the soil food web. They help with the decomposition process, breaking down leaves and animal matter so their energy can return to the soil.

Plants feed their sugars to a large community of bacteria and fungi that gather at their roots. The bacteria chow down on that as well as decomposing leaves.

They also attract larger predators like nematodes, which leave behind nutrient-dense waste.

This partnership between plants and bacteria benefits them both!

WHAT'S THAT SOIL SMELL?

Why does it smell so earthy when it rains? It's all thanks to one type of soil bacteria, streptomyces (strep-toe-MY-cees). This bacterium produces a chemical that creates that familiar earthy smell, called geosmin. Geosmin is like catnip to small creatures called springtails and attracts them to the bacteria. The springtails will feed on the bacteria and carry bacterial spores with them to distribute far and wide.

AH, WHAT A WONDERFUL AROMA. LET'S EAT!

Plenty of Protozoa

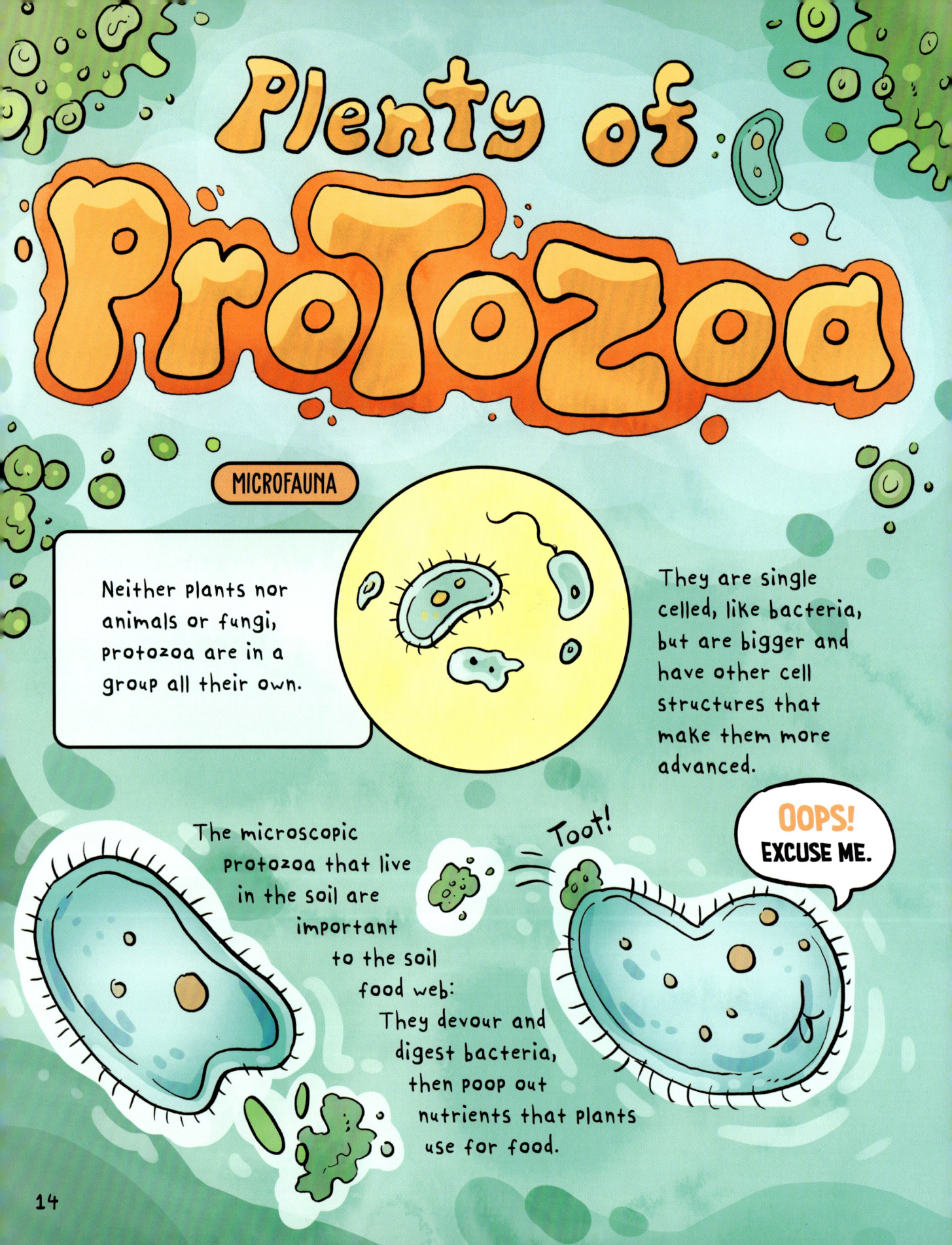

MICROFAUNA

Neither plants nor animals or fungi, protozoa are in a group all their own.

They are single celled, like bacteria, but are bigger and have other cell structures that make them more advanced.

The microscopic protozoa that live in the soil are important to the soil food web: They devour and digest bacteria, then poop out nutrients that plants use for food.

Toot!

OOPS! EXCUSE ME.

There are different types of protozoa, which are named according to how they get around:

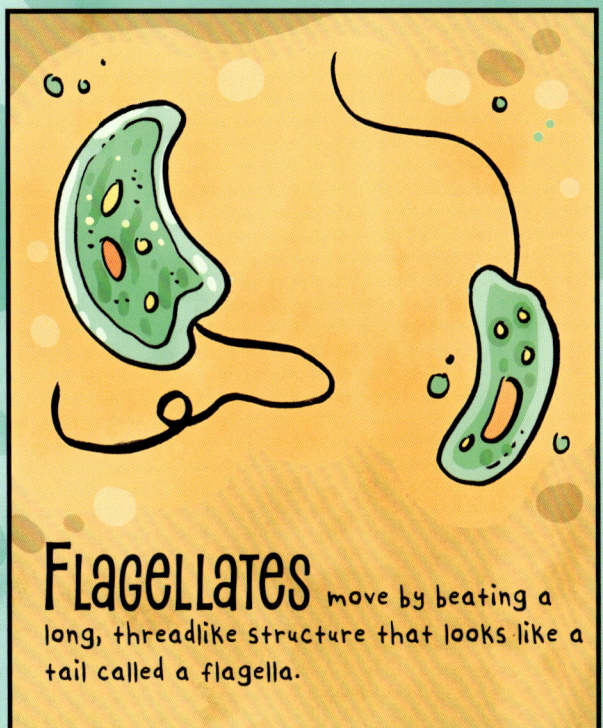

Flagellates
move by beating a long, threadlike structure that looks like a tail called a flagella.

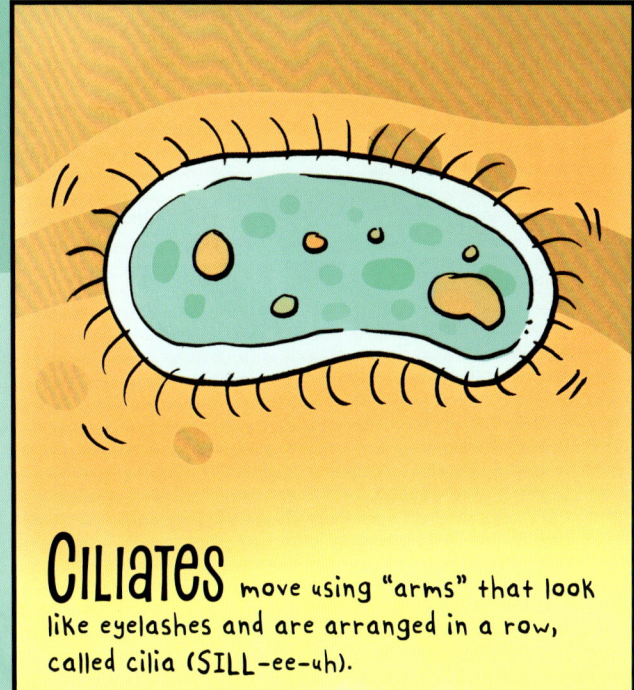

Ciliates
move using "arms" that look like eyelashes and are arranged in a row, called cilia (SILL-ee-uh).

Amoebas
move using pseudopods (SUE-doh-pods), which is Latin for "false feet." These fake feet can move and change shape, and amoeboid protozoa use them to hunt and capture prey.

Sporozoans
do not actually move around on their own.

They are parasites that live inside a host organism. One type of sporozoan is well known for causing the dangerous disease malaria, which lives in mosquitoes—the hosts in this instance—and is then transferred to humans when they're bitten.

NEMATODE: Friend or Foe?

MICROFAUNA

Nematodes (also called roundworms) are one of the most numerous animals in the soil. In fact, they make up 80 percent of all animal life on earth! (But they are usually very tiny, and most species are only the width of a human hair.)

Some are helpful to the soil habitat, some are harmful, and some feed on root juices while others are predators that eat other soil microfauna.

But many animals eat nematodes. The large number of nematodes in the soil becomes a bountiful noodley buffet for everything from springtails to flatworms.

Sluuurp!

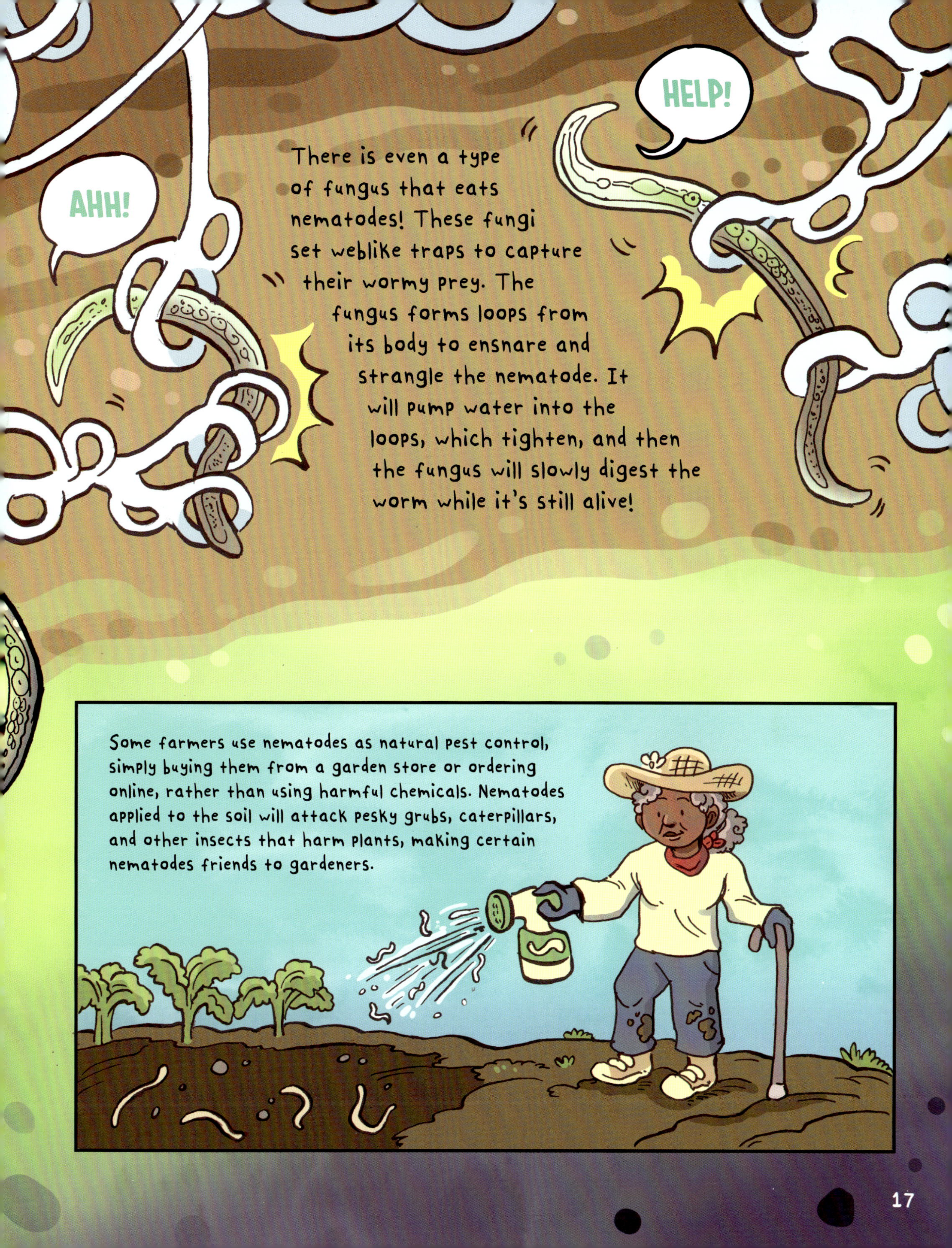
AHH!
HELP!
There is even a type of fungus that eats nematodes! These fungi set weblike traps to capture their wormy prey. The fungus forms loops from its body to ensnare and strangle the nematode. It will pump water into the loops, which tighten, and then the fungus will slowly digest the worm while it's still alive!
Some farmers use nematodes as natural pest control, simply buying them from a garden store or ordering online, rather than using harmful chemicals. Nematodes applied to the soil will attack pesky grubs, caterpillars, and other insects that harm plants, making certain nematodes friends to gardeners.

Fabulous Fungus

The mushrooms you see on the surface of your lawn are just a small part of a much larger fungus organism. It is in fact the networks of underground roots that make up the majority of the fungus.

MICROFAUNA

Mushrooms are the way the fungus releases spores to reproduce.

After release, the spores take root in the ground and reach out in tendrils called hyphae (HIGH-fee).

These branching webs of hundreds of tendrils are called a mycorrhizal (migh-koh-RIGH-zuhl) network.

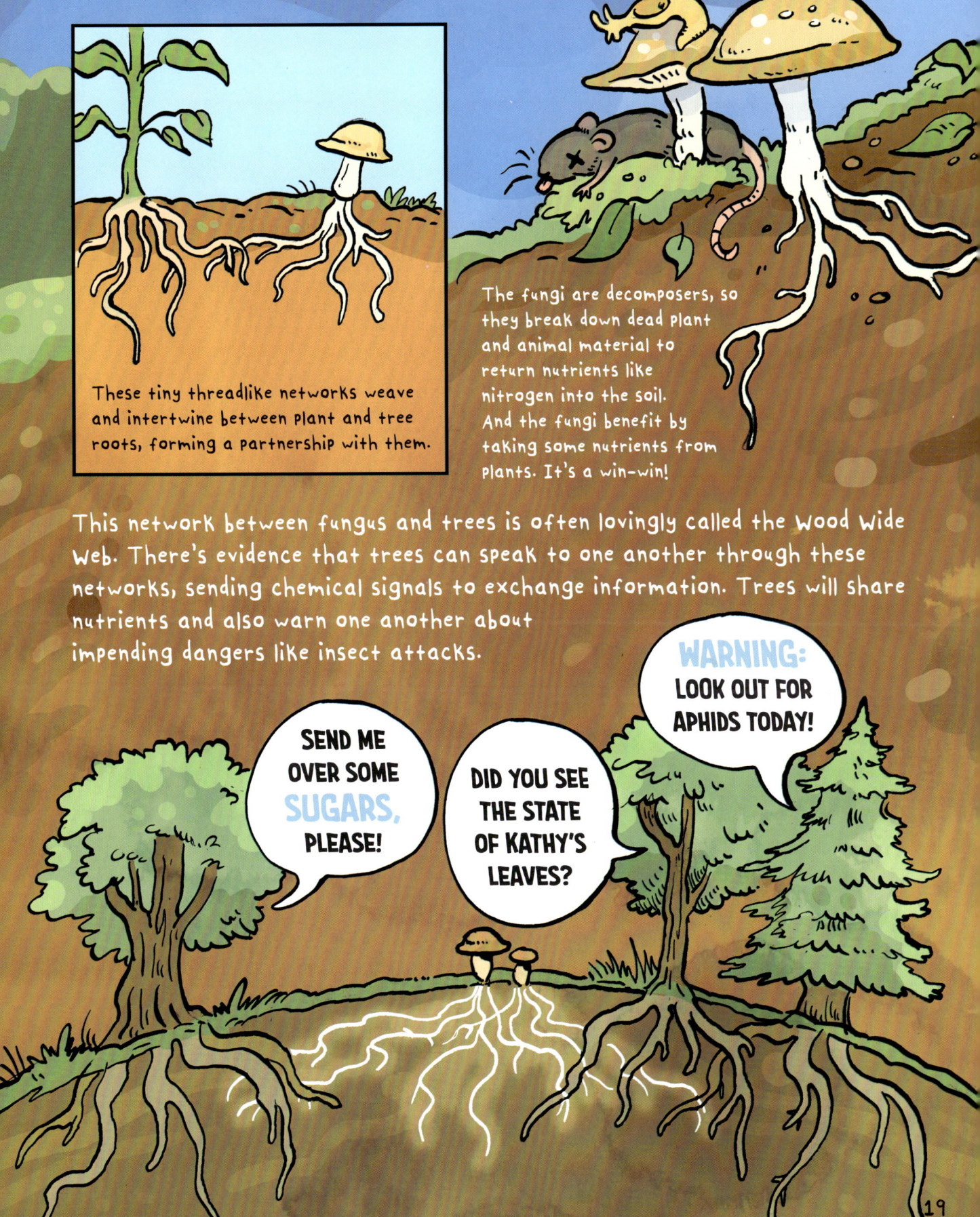

These tiny threadlike networks weave and intertwine between plant and tree roots, forming a partnership with them.

The fungi are decomposers, so they break down dead plant and animal material to return nutrients like nitrogen into the soil. And the fungi benefit by taking some nutrients from plants. It's a win-win!

This network between fungus and trees is often lovingly called the Wood Wide Web. There's evidence that trees can speak to one another through these networks, sending chemical signals to exchange information. Trees will share nutrients and also warn one another about impending dangers like insect attacks.

SEND ME OVER SOME SUGARS, PLEASE!

DID YOU SEE THE STATE OF KATHY'S LEAVES?

WARNING: LOOK OUT FOR APHIDS TODAY!

RADICAL ROTIFERS

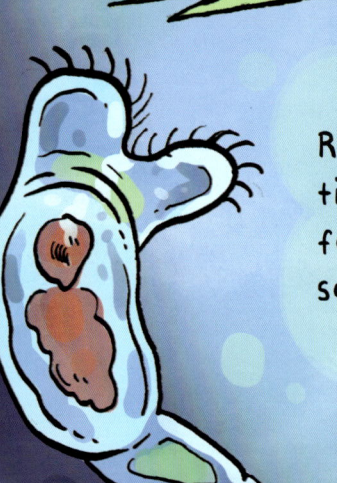

Rotifers are very strange-looking, tiny animals. They're mostly known for dwelling in ponds and lakes, but some live in soil.

MICROFAUNA

Their name means "wheel bearers" because they have beating cilia at the top of their heads that look like a wheel turning.

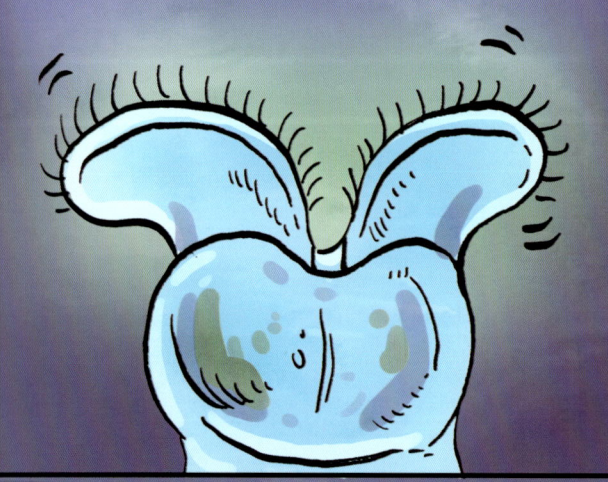

They use the cilia to suck algae into their mouths.

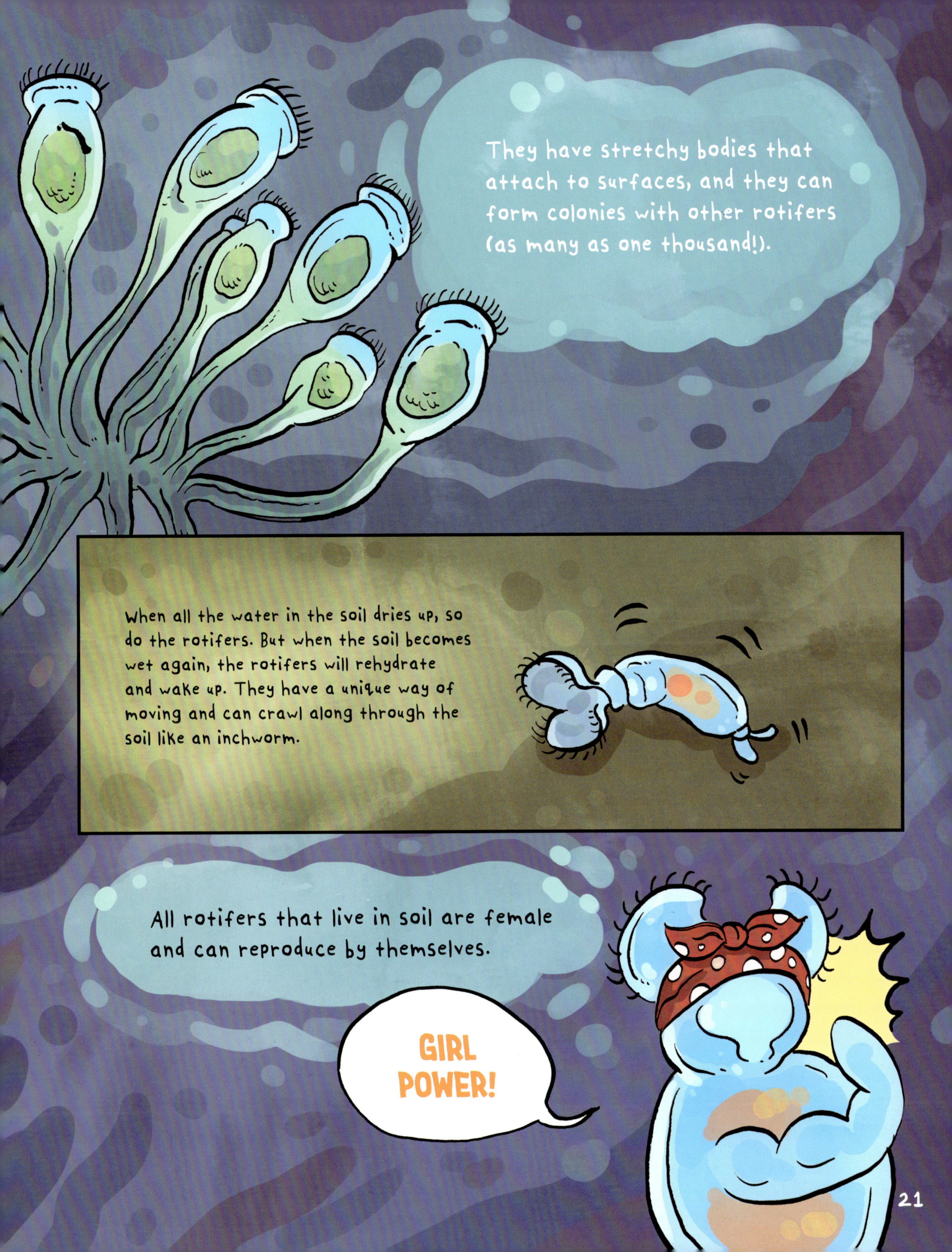
They have stretchy bodies that attach to surfaces, and they can form colonies with other rotifers (as many as one thousand!).
When all the water in the soil dries up, so do the rotifers. But when the soil becomes wet again, the rotifers will rehydrate and wake up. They have a unique way of moving and can crawl along through the soil like an inchworm.
All rotifers that live in soil are female and can reproduce by themselves.
GIRL POWER!

Slithering SLIME MOLDS

Slime molds move through the soil and leaf litter like the Blob or a movie monster, gobbling up bacteria. Slime molds may look like fungus, but they are really a type of amoeboid protozoa (a type of single-celled organism). There are two different types of slime mold: cellular and plasmodial.

Plasmodial slime molds can be seen without a microscope and they swarm together to form a multi-cellular organism.

Cellular slime molds can only be seen with a microscope. They stay as single cells throughout their lives and call on other slime mold cells to help find food.

WHO ARE YOU CALLING **BRAINLESS?**

Although they are brainless, slime molds are shockingly smart! As they roam the forest floor, slime mold cells make complex choices about where to go and how to find food. They can learn and retain memories of where food is located. In experiments, scientists have observed slime molds navigating mazes and even creating a replica of the Tokyo rail system.

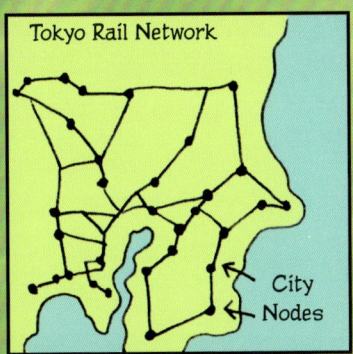

Tokyo Rail Network

City Nodes

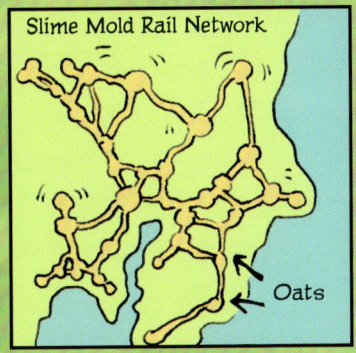

Slime Mold Rail Network

Oats

When scientists placed oats in a dish at points that represented the thirty-six cities connected by the rail network, the slime mold cleverly mapped out a route to the oats in a way that looked almost exactly like the rail system, and in certain areas, it found more efficient, shorter routes between cities.

Maybe the next time a city needs public transport, they can hire a professional slime mold to design it!

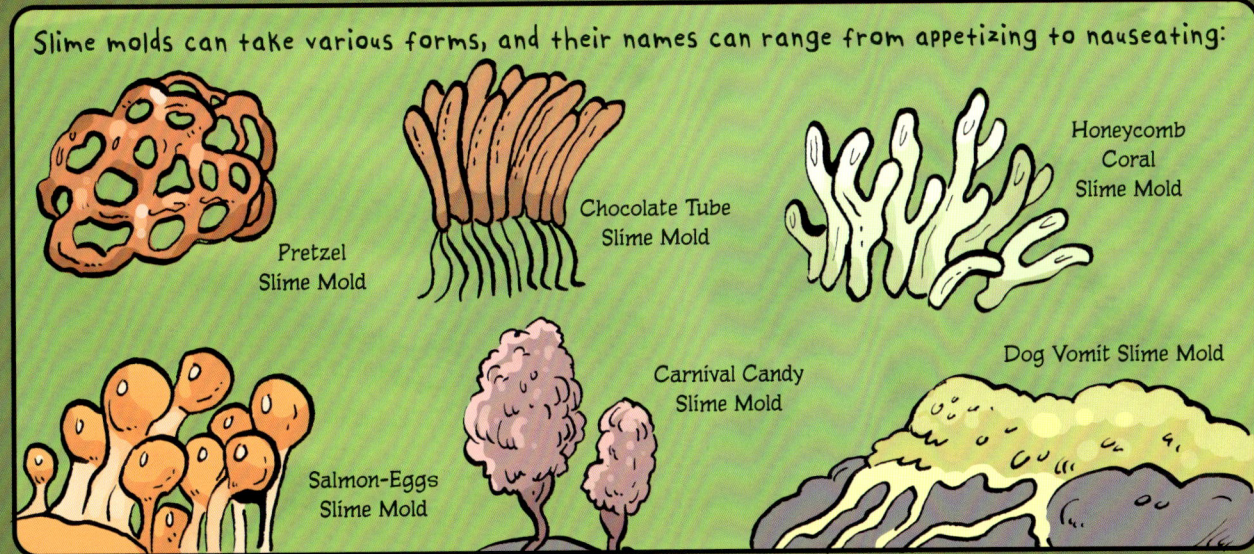

Slime molds can take various forms, and their names can range from appetizing to nauseating:

Pretzel Slime Mold

Chocolate Tube Slime Mold

Honeycomb Coral Slime Mold

Salmon-Eggs Slime Mold

Carnival Candy Slime Mold

Dog Vomit Slime Mold

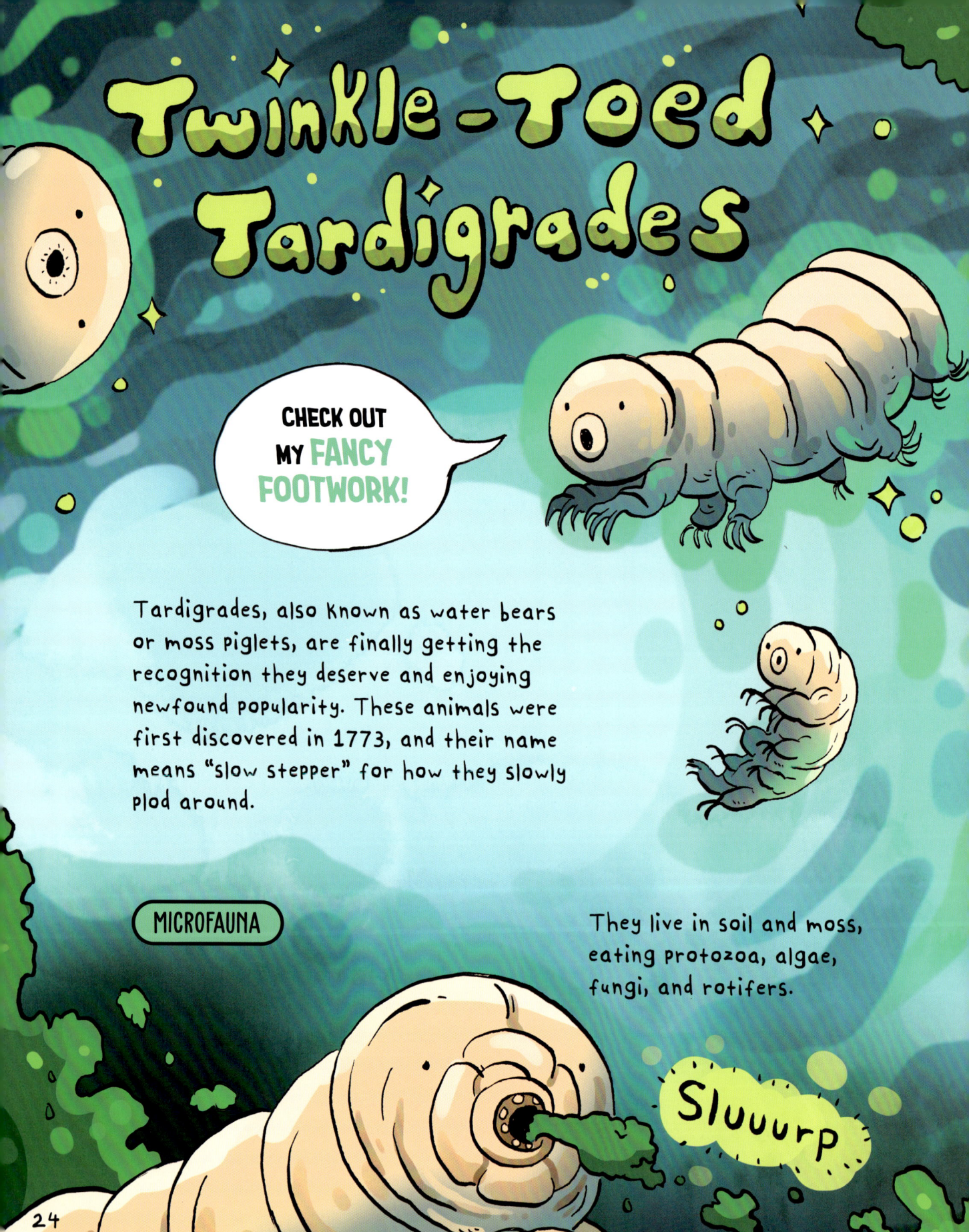

Twinkle-Toed Tardigrades

CHECK OUT MY **FANCY FOOTWORK!**

Tardigrades, also known as water bears or moss piglets, are finally getting the recognition they deserve and enjoying newfound popularity. These animals were first discovered in 1773, and their name means "slow stepper" for how they slowly plod around.

MICROFAUNA

They live in soil and moss, eating protozoa, algae, fungi, and rotifers.

Sluuurp

These unassuming creatures have amazing superpowers: They can withstand intense cold, nuclear radiation, and even the lifeless vacuum of space!

Ka Boom!

COME IN, HOUSTON...

They do this by drying out their bodies and going into a state called cryptobiosis (crip-toe-bye-OH-sis). They become dehydrated like a cracker, and in this form, they can withstand almost anything. Like rotifers, when they are rehydrated with water, they spring back to life.

YOU CAN'T KEEP A GOOD TARDIGRADE DOWN!

z z z

Dehydrated

A dried-out museum specimen of moss containing tardigrades was left alone for 120 years. And when it was rehydrated, the tardigrades within it also woke up from their long nap.

This might lead you to believe that tardigrades are immortal and indestructible, but they can be killed like any other creature. They're particularly vulnerable to hot temperatures, especially hot water.

HUH...? WHAT YEAR IS IT?

NOOO... HOT WATER, MY ONLY WEAKNESS!

Awesome Algae

MICROFLORA

Algae are plantlike organisms that are commonly found in the water, but they can live in soil as well (even soils found in the desert!). They are great contributors to the soil community.

Using photosynthesis like a plant, they take in the sun's rays and generously add organic matter to the soil, keeping it healthy and keeping the animals that live in the soil well-fed.

THANKS, ALGAE!

and Lichens

Lichen = Algae + Fungal hyphae

Lichens are a combination of two organisms: algae and soil fungi.

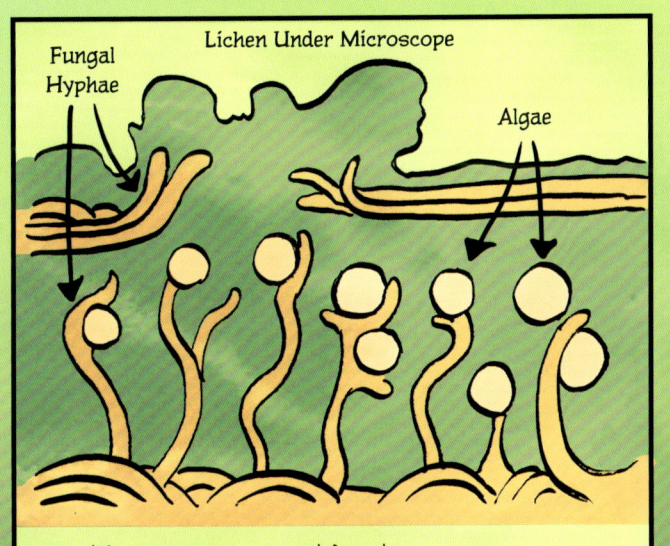

Lichen Under Microscope

Fungal Hyphae

Algae

In this equal partnership, the fungus creates the body of the lichen, and the algae provide organic nutrients obtained through photosynthesis. It's one of the few organisms that can survive on solid rock!

Together, the algae and fungi can survive harsher conditions than they ever could on their own, like freezing temperatures, harsh sunlight, and droughts.

STICK WITH ME, BUDDY!

TEAMWORK MAKES THE DREAM WORK!

Soil Mesofauna: Less Tiny, Still Mighty!

Mesofauna are a small step up in size from microfauna. They can be seen without a microscope, but only barely: Many are still very small (only between 0.004 and 0.08 inches long), which is about the size of a grain of sand. This group includes mites and springtails, both of which are very plentiful.

YOU PROBABLY HAVEN'T NOTICED BUT...

Mite

WE ARE EVERYWHERE!

Springtail

Soil mesofauna can be found on every continent in the world, even Antarctica! They're important because they contribute to the soil food web. Most mesofauna hang out in the upper layer of soil and leaf litter, and by munching on that leaf litter, they help the decomposition process. Breaking down organic matter makes soil healthier for everyone.

MIGHTY MITES

Mites are another numerous and important part of the soil food web and producers of humus. Mites are very tiny arachnids—a group of invertebrates (animals without a backbone) with eight legs that includes spiders and ticks.

Spider

Oribatid mite

Tick

Soil mites are great for the health of the soil. They play an important role in the soil food web by breaking down all sorts of dead material to help the soil to become more nutritious for the critters that live there.

Oribatid mites, also called moss mites or beetle mites, are one of the most numerous of any arthropod (invertebrates with a segmented body such as insects, spiders, crabs, and millipedes) in forest soil, feeding on fungi, wood, and algae. Oribatid mites also have a hard shell (like a beetle) to protect themselves from predators.

MESOFAUNA

They can be found in soils all over the world, from forests to deserts to wetlands. They're so tiny, they only move a few feet during their entire lifetime! But they can hitch a ride on other creatures.

WE'RE OFF TO SEE THE WORLD!

A-bounding Springtails

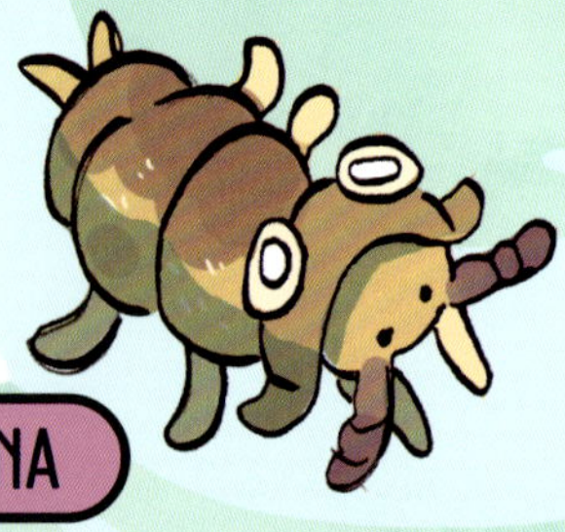

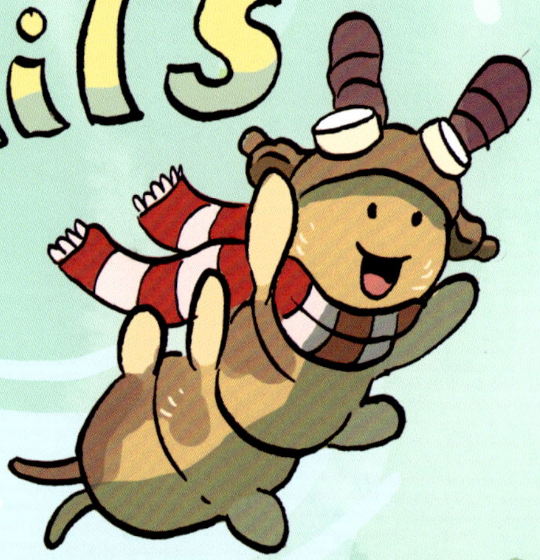

MESOFAUNA

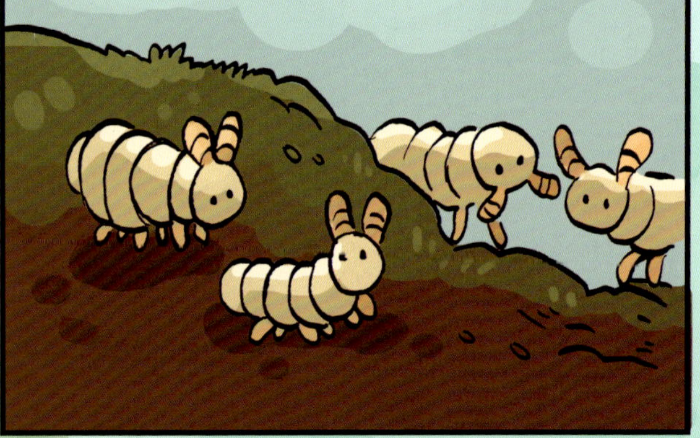

Springtails are one of the most abundant types of mesofauna.

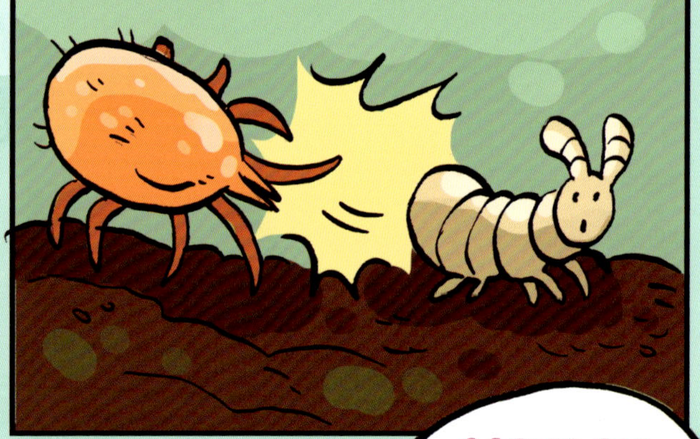

Plenty of other soil animals, like mites, rely on springtails for their dinner! But springtails have plenty to offer besides their taste.

These teeny arthropods have the incredible ability to take flight. But with no wings, how do they get airborne? Many types of springtails can vault into the air using a fork-shaped organ called a furcula that they can flick to spring upward.

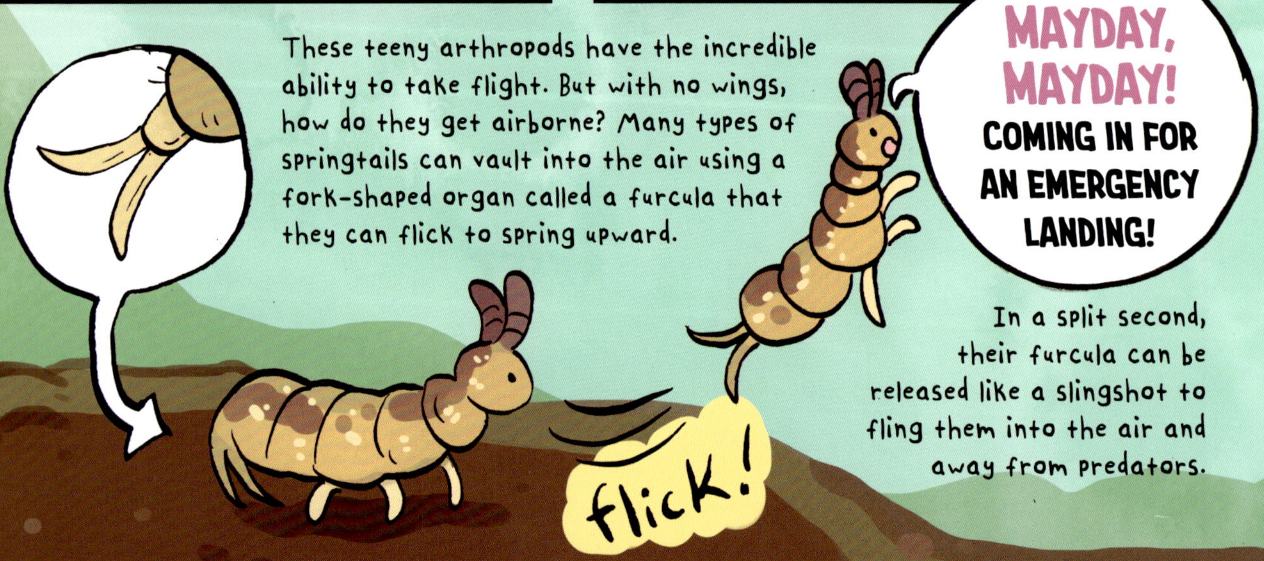
MAYDAY, MAYDAY! COMING IN FOR AN EMERGENCY LANDING!
flick!

In a split second, their furcula can be released like a slingshot to fling them into the air and away from predators.

They come in so many different shapes, forms, and colors, too.

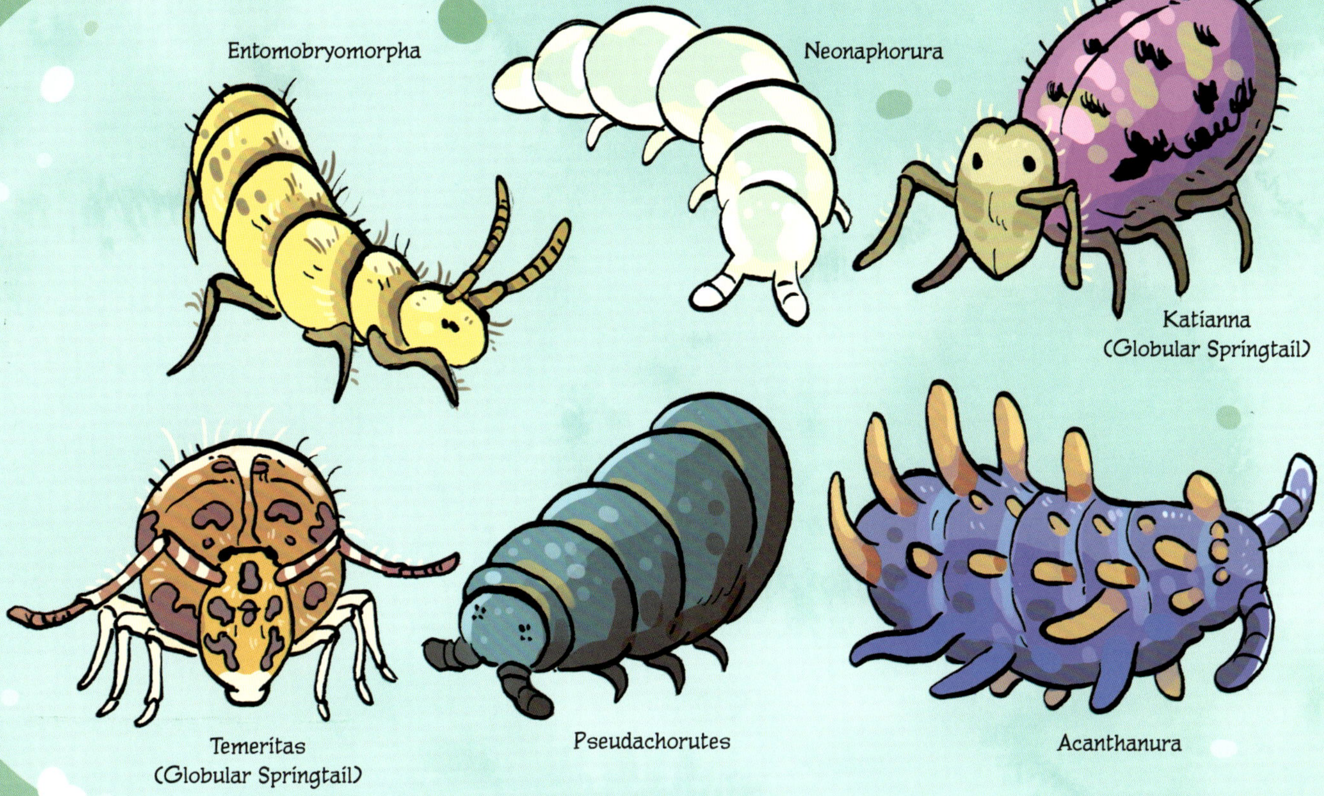
Entomobryomorpha
Neonaphorura
Katianna
(Globular Springtail)
Temeritas
(Globular Springtail)
Pseudachorutes
Acanthanura

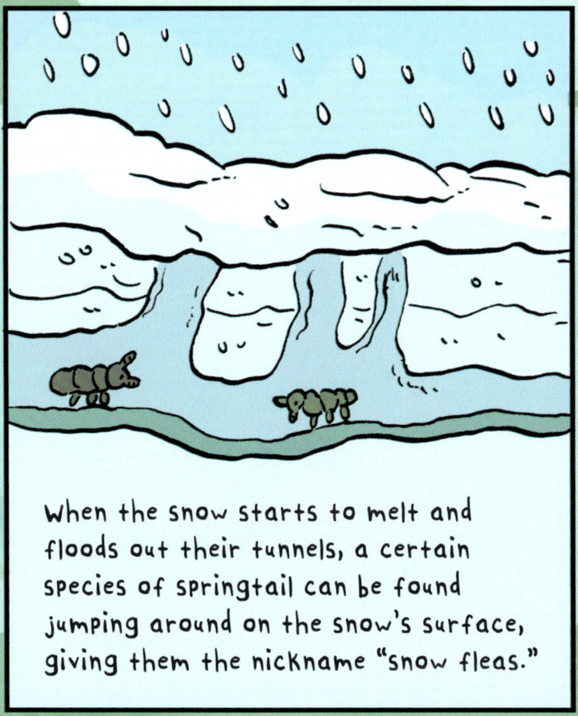
When the snow starts to melt and floods out their tunnels, a certain species of springtail can be found jumping around on the snow's surface, giving them the nickname "snow fleas."

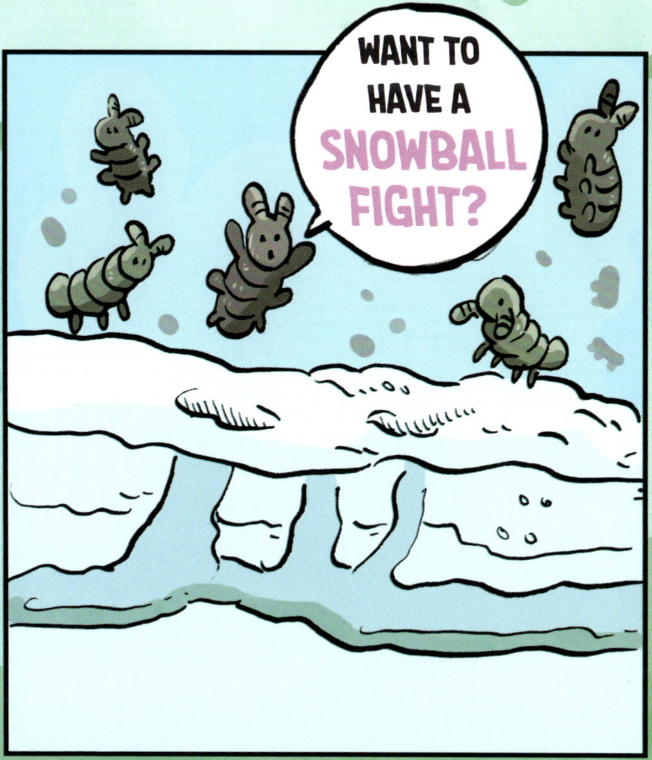
WANT TO HAVE A SNOWBALL FIGHT?

A MESOFAUNA

MESOFAUNA

The Garden Centipede

The garden centipede is so small, it fits through little gaps and holes in the soil to feed on plant roots. They use their large antennae to find their way around the soil.

Pauropods

Pauropods are a type of tiny animal. One type of pauropod has three sets of legs when born, but they gain legs as they grow and can have as many as eleven sets of legs as an adult. They use their mouthparts to groom themselves, like a cat or dog!

MEOW!

Proturans

Proturans are also called coneheads. They spend their time eating decaying organic matter. They carry their two front legs, which are used as sensing tools, raised like antennae.

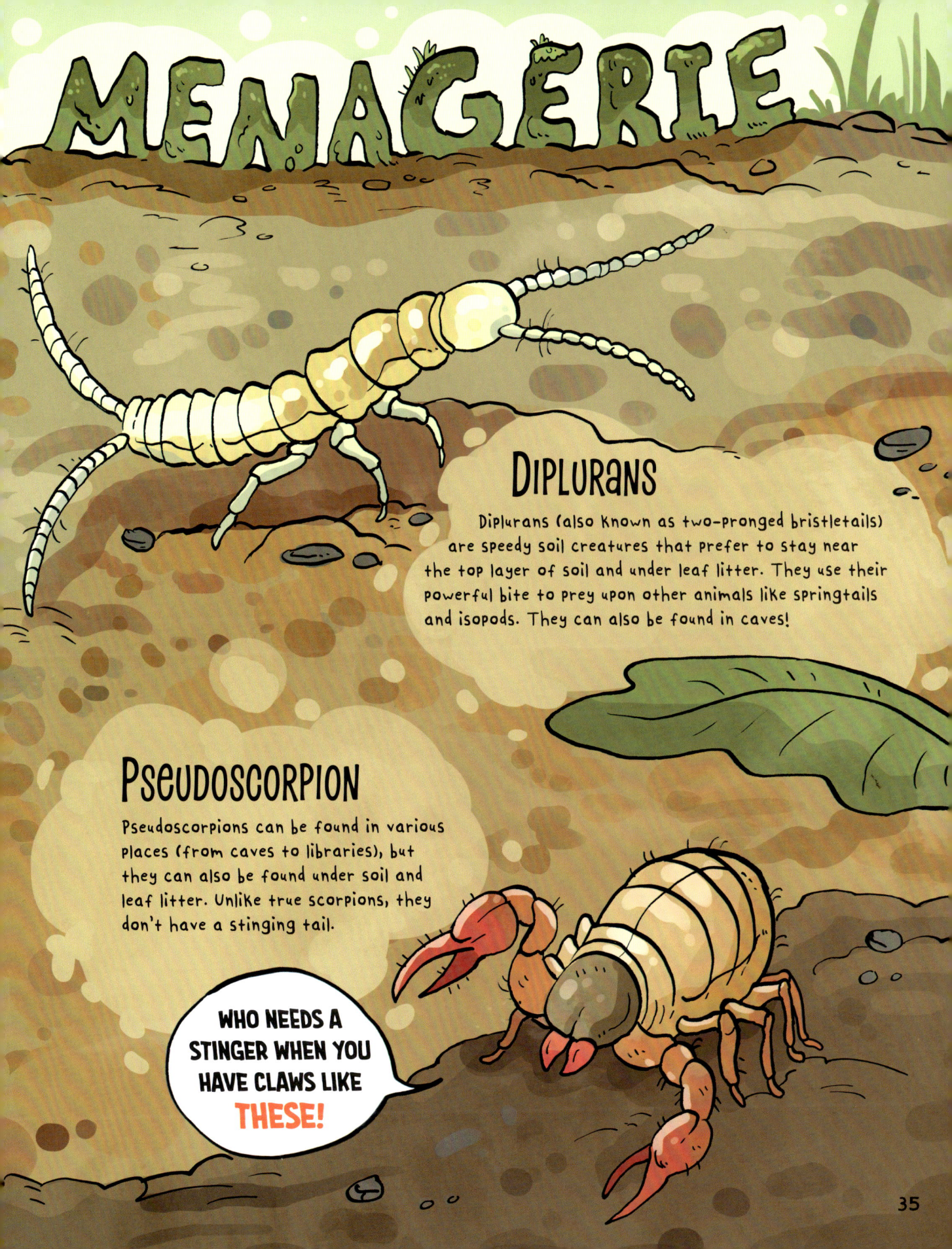

MENAGERIE

Diplurans

Diplurans (also known as two-pronged bristletails) are speedy soil creatures that prefer to stay near the top layer of soil and under leaf litter. They use their powerful bite to prey upon other animals like springtails and isopods. They can also be found in caves!

Pseudoscorpion

Pseudoscorpions can be found in various places (from caves to libraries), but they can also be found under soil and leaf litter. Unlike true scorpions, they don't have a stinging tail.

WHO NEEDS A STINGER WHEN YOU HAVE CLAWS LIKE THESE!

Soil Macrofauna: Creepy-Crawlies

Macrofauna are a little bigger but no longer than an inch. Most of these critters are a type of invertebrate such as insects, arachnids, and worms.

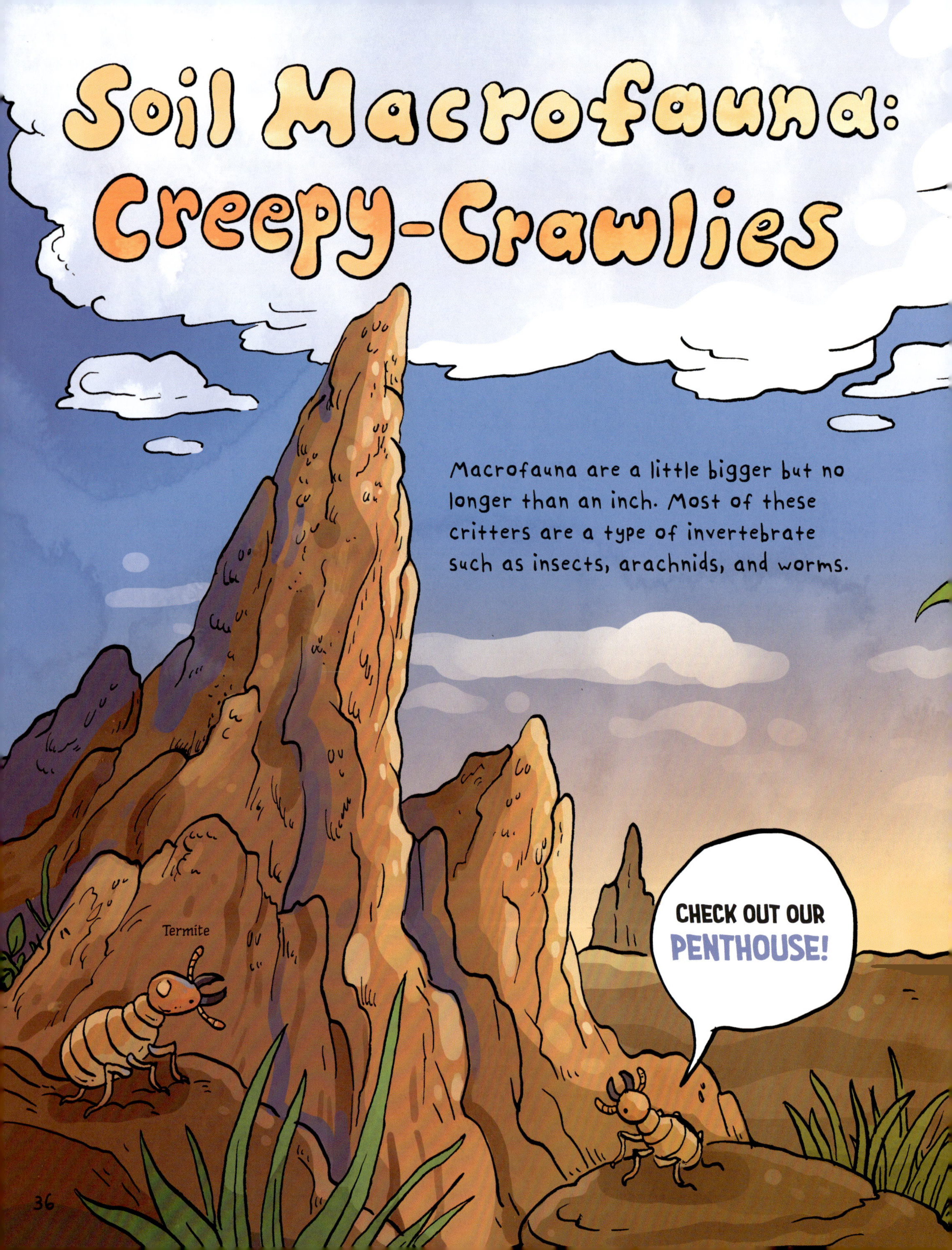
Termite
CHECK OUT OUR PENTHOUSE!

SO LONG, SOIL!

Cicada

Macrofauna, like woodlice and earthworms, are great contributors to the health of the soil, helping to return nutrients to it by decomposing leaf litter. And others, like cicadas and antlions, live part of their life cycle underground, and then emerge ready to take to the skies!

Ant

Woodlouse

Millipede

Antlion

Centipede

Earthworm

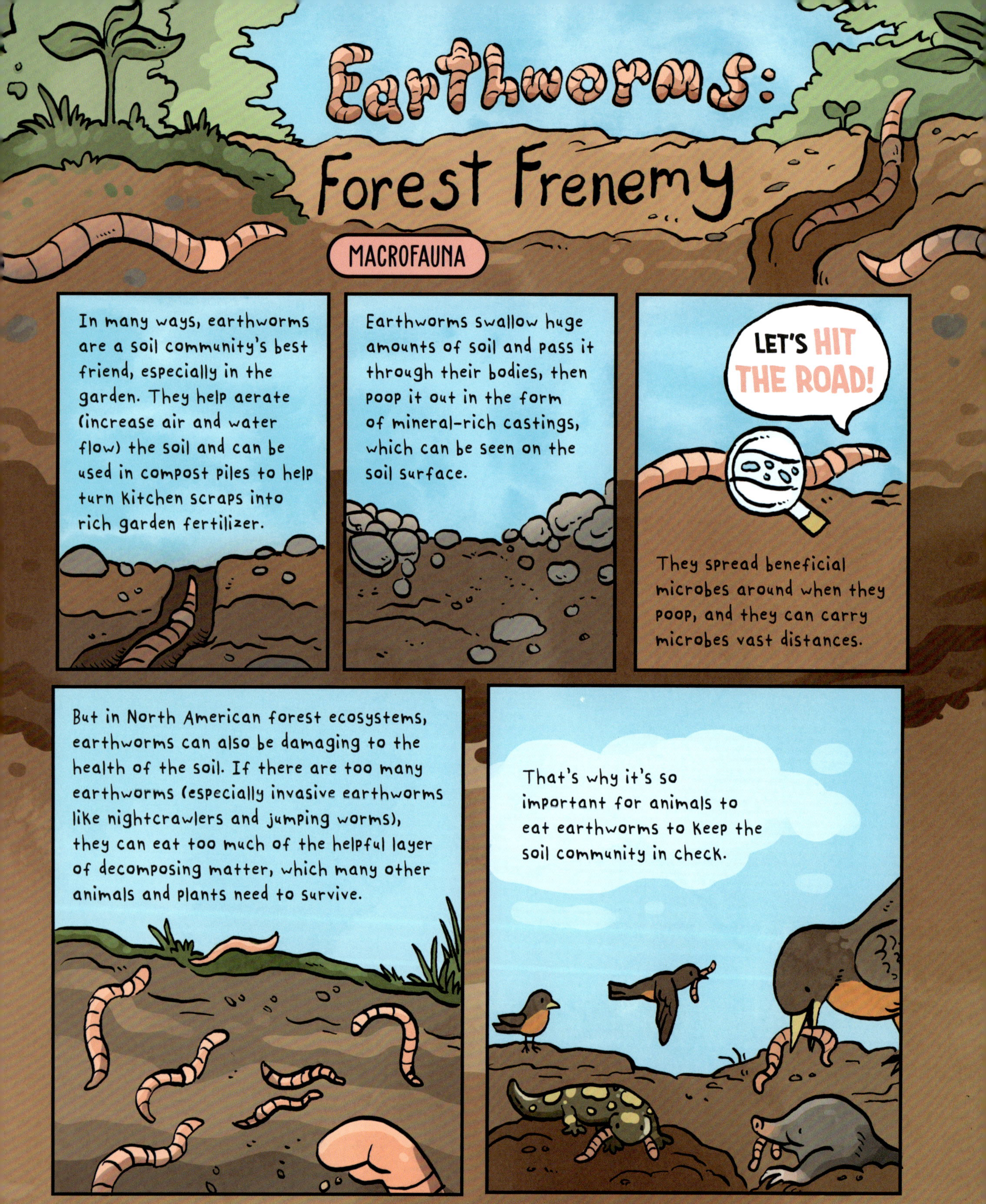
Earthworms:
Forest Frenemy
MACROFAUNA
In many ways, earthworms are a soil community's best friend, especially in the garden. They help aerate (increase air and water flow) the soil and can be used in compost piles to help turn kitchen scraps into rich garden fertilizer.
Earthworms swallow huge amounts of soil and pass it through their bodies, then poop it out in the form of mineral-rich castings, which can be seen on the soil surface.
LET'S HIT THE ROAD!
They spread beneficial microbes around when they poop, and they can carry microbes vast distances.
But in North American forest ecosystems, earthworms can also be damaging to the health of the soil. If there are too many earthworms (especially invasive earthworms like nightcrawlers and jumping worms), they can eat too much of the helpful layer of decomposing matter, which many other animals and plants need to survive.
That's why it's so important for animals to eat earthworms to keep the soil community in check.

Earthworms are missing a lot of typical animal body parts, but they manage just fine.

Without teeth, earthworms swallow stones that help them grind up food particles in a part of their body called the gizzard.

Without lungs, earthworms breathe through their skin, which they need to keep moist.

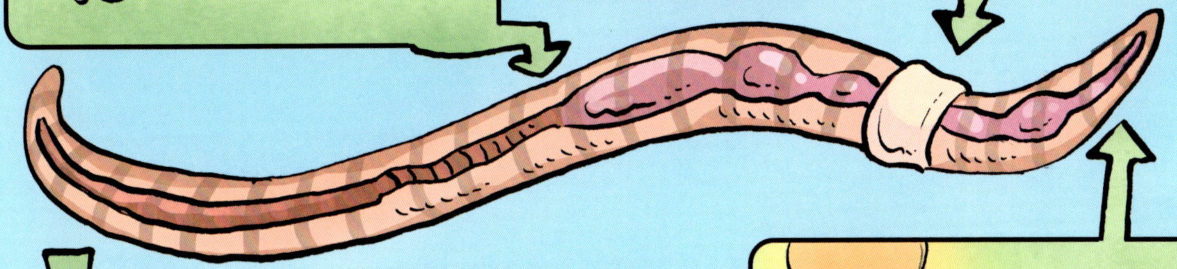

Without legs, they use muscles and tiny bristles on their segmented bodies to move through the soil.

Though they have no eyes, they have light-sensing cells at the top of their head that can detect when their surroundings are in light or darkness.

There are more varieties of earthworms than you might expect, from the green worm (earthworms that come in a light shade of green) to the giant Gippsland earthworm from Australia, which has been known to grow to nine feet in length!

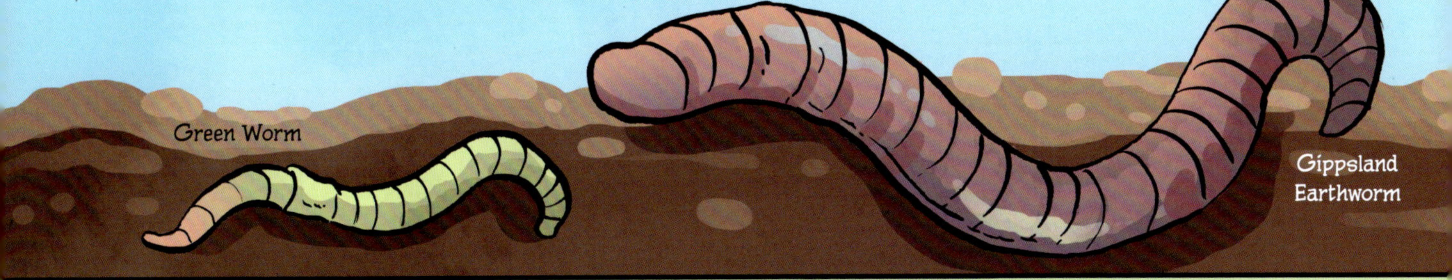
Green Worm
Gippsland Earthworm

Slippery Stowaways!

Almost all earthworms in North America are immigrants! Melting glaciers drowned native North American earthworm species around ten thousand years ago. So the earthworms that are currently found in the US came from other places like Europe and Asia as stowaways in the soil of potted plants and in the ballasts of ships—the heavy material, like rocks and soil, that is put in the bottom of a ship to keep it more stable.

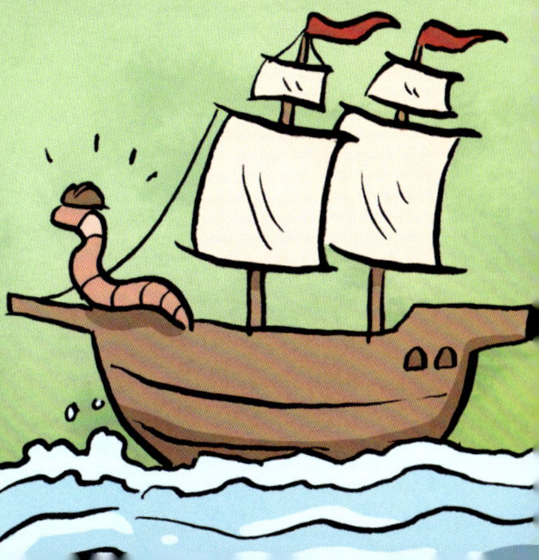

More Wonderful

Flatworms

Flatworms are a simple animal, with no respiratory (breathing) or circulatory (blood flow) systems. One type of flatworm, called planarians, has only one opening in their gut, called a pharynx, which can extend out from its body to suck up food. The pharynx acts as a mouth as well as an opening for excreting waste.

IT'S A
TWO FOR ONE!

Some of them have tiny eyespots on their heads, and some have small eyespots speckling their sides. Flatworm eyespots are much more basic than our eyes, and they can see only light rather than visual details.

Flatworms don't burrow but instead glide on top of the soil, slipping and sliding over leaf litter.

Hammerhead flatworms have the same deadly toxin (a poison called tetrodotoxin) that pufferfish have. They use this toxin to hunt, rubbing their heads and bodies over earthworms to stun them, so the hammerhead worm can liquefy and slurp up the earthworm's insides.

WORMS

RIBBON WORMS

Nemerteans, also known as ribbon worms, live mostly in water, but some live on land. Their most notable feature is their ability to spew out a part of their body called their proboscis (like a nose), which looks like a pile of noodles but has a venomous sting. Like slugs and snails, they scoot around on a trail of mucus.

POTWORMS

Potworms resemble tiny whitish earthworms (they're called potworms because they often live in potted garden plants). They too contribute to the health of the soil by both helping to decompose matter and by burrowing. Their burrows make the soil more porous (meaning full of holes), so there is more space for water to reach and bacteria to grow.

Certain species of potworms live in glaciers and are called ice worms! These potworms will dine on algae growing in the ice.

Ambitious Ants

A LITTLE TO THE LEFT...

HOLD IT STEADY!

Ants have many occupations: They are engineers, soldiers, and even farmers. They are called eusocial (you-SOH-shul), which means they live in a complex society where everyone has a role to play. There is usually one special female in the group that can have babies. She is called the queen.

In the soil, ants construct intricate nests full of tunnels and chambers. They can move tons of soil (and other objects many times their own body weight!). Some chambers are for storing food, some are for eggs and raising larvae (the baby form of an insect), and the queen even gets her very own throne room.

Some ants are fungus farmers! Leafcutter ants harvest parts of leaves and then bring them back to their nests. Some might think that the leafcutter ants gobble up the leaves themselves, but they really use this leaf material to grow a specific type of fungus. This fungus is the leafcutter ants' preferred source of food.

But like any farmer, leafcutter ants must battle with pests to preserve the health of their garden.

ONLY **MUSHROOMS** FOR US, NO SALAD.

Escovopsis

TIME TO **DISINFECT** THE NEST.

When a parasitic fungus (parasitic organisms live in or on another organism and cause it harm) called *Escovopsis* infiltrates their garden, the ants team up with a helpful bacteria called *Pseudonocardia* (soo-don-oh-card-eeah) to rid the garden of the pest. The "good" bacteria produce antibiotics that hang out on the ant's body and help rid the colony of invasive fungus spores.

Not Your Average Ant Farm

Ants aren't only fungus farmers; some species of ants also add livestock management to their résumé! They have a relationship with smaller insects called aphids. The ants herd and protect the aphids, and they even milk the aphids by stroking them with their antennae to get them to release a sweet substance called honeydew, which the ants lap up.

HOME, HOME ON THE RANGE... WHERE THE APHIDS AND ANTLIONS PLAY...

Towering Termites

Many termites are known for eating through the wooden parts of human houses and other buildings. But the mound-building termites are soil engineers! The towering termite mounds can be found in Africa, South America, Asia, and Australia, and they are a testament to termites' building power. Forget bricks and concrete, these skyscrapers are made from soil, saliva, and dung.

Termite CITY

Population: 1,000,000

Queen

Worker

Soldier

BREAK TIME'S OVER, **BACK TO WORK!**

Like ants, termites are also eusocial. They live in societies of workers, soldiers, and a queen.

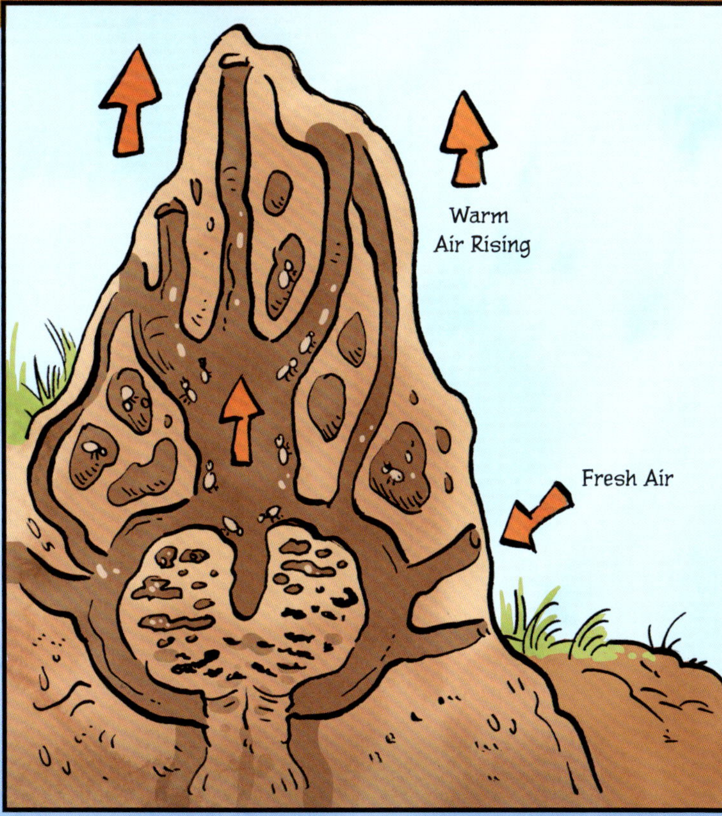

Warm Air Rising

Fresh Air

Termite mounds are climate-controlled! Because mound-building termites live in some of the hottest places in the world, their mounds are well ventilated so that they can keep cool. Scientists are still trying to understand how termite tunnels control air flow. Perhaps we can use termite structures as a model to create climate-controlled buildings without air-conditioning for humans.

AHHHHHHHH! ANTLIONS!

It's a quiet day in the dirt, and an unsuspecting insect is toddling along enjoying the breeze...

MACROFAUNA

All of a sudden, it slips! It plummets into a sandy pit. Unable to get out, it struggles and struggles and then SNAP!! Huge jaws erupt out of the sandy soil and crunch up the unlucky insect. This is the formidable munching mouth of the antlion!

I'M JUST A WIDDLE BABY! NOT A **DEADLY PREDATOR,** NOT ME!

The antlion is the larva of an antlion lacewing. While in its infant stage, the antlion creates traps to catch prey. It is covered in sensitive bristles that can sense movements in the sand and judge when to attack.

When the antlion is mature enough, it will build a cocoon and develop inside it. Then it will emerge as a delicate antlion lacewing.

Losing the huge jaws of its youth, some adult antlions eat other insects, while some only eat nectar and pollen.

WANT TO SEE MY BABY PICTURES? I HAD A REAL **GLOW UP,** DON'T YOU THINK?

Slow and Steady: Snails and Slugs

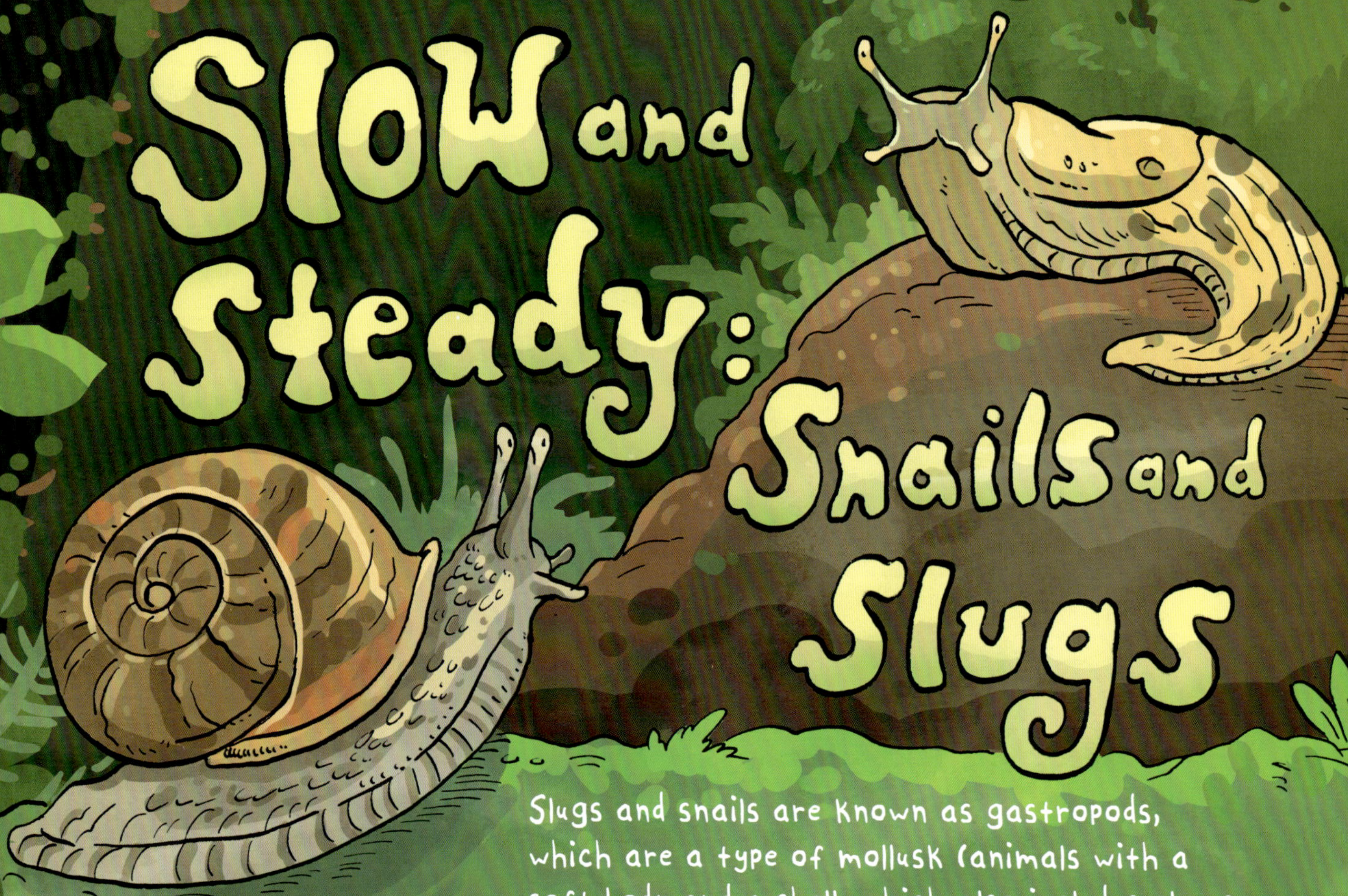

MACROFAUNA

Slugs and snails are known as gastropods, which are a type of mollusk (animals with a soft body and a shell, which also includes clams, oysters, squid, and octopuses).

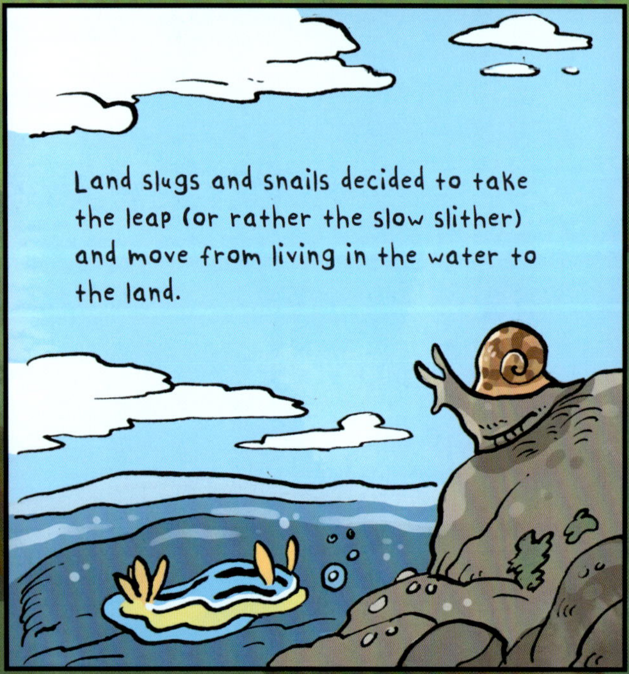
Land slugs and snails decided to take the leap (or rather the slow slither) and move from living in the water to the land.

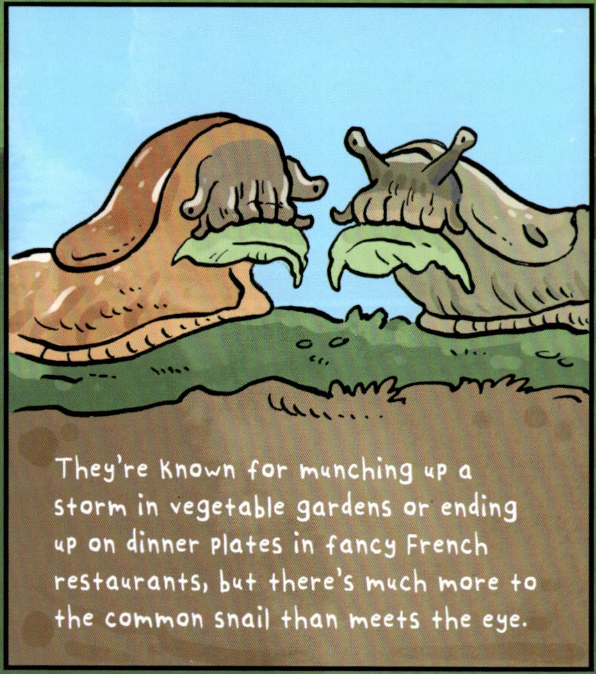
They're known for munching up a storm in vegetable gardens or ending up on dinner plates in fancy French restaurants, but there's much more to the common snail than meets the eye.

Snails and slugs move around on one muscular foot, which secretes a mucus that helps them slide and also protects them from being hurt by any sharp objects in the soil. This mucus leaves a gleaming snail trail behind it as the snail explores the soil.

Foot

Snails and slugs have a special mouthpart called a radula, which looks a bit like a cheese grater when viewed under a microscope. It helps them grate and scrape up food.

Radula

What's the difference between slugs and snails? Clearly, it seems that snails have shells and slugs do not, but snails came first, and then slugs evolved from snails. Many slugs still have a small internal shell. Both animals have different advantages: Snails can retract and hide in their shells from predators, and slugs can squeeze into smaller areas that snails cannot.

I'M SOOO JEALOUS...

Not a Slug, Not a Snail, but a SEMI-SLUG!

A semi-slug (sometimes known as a snug!) is in between a slug and snail. They have a less developed outside shell that is not big enough to hide in.

The Trapdoor Spider:
Masters of Disguise and Surprise

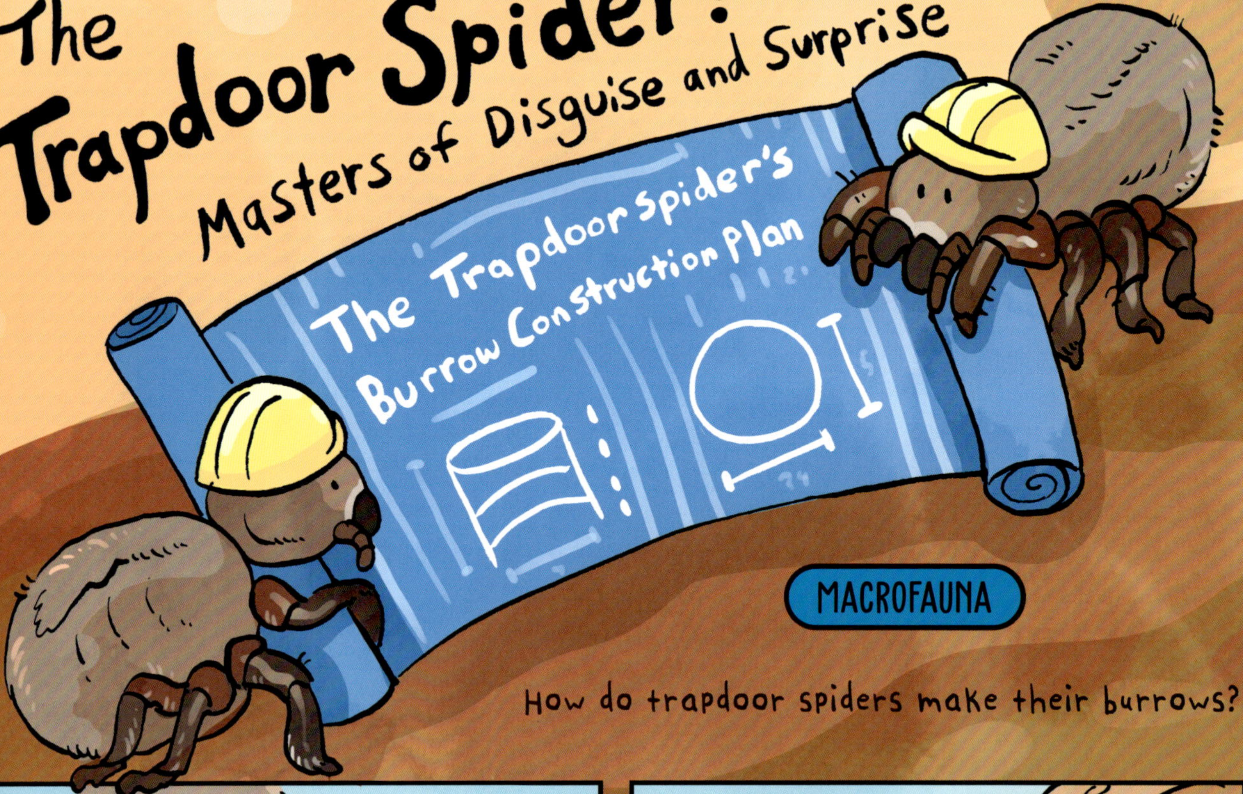
The Trapdoor Spider's
Burrow Construction Plan

MACROFAUNA

How do trapdoor spiders make their burrows?

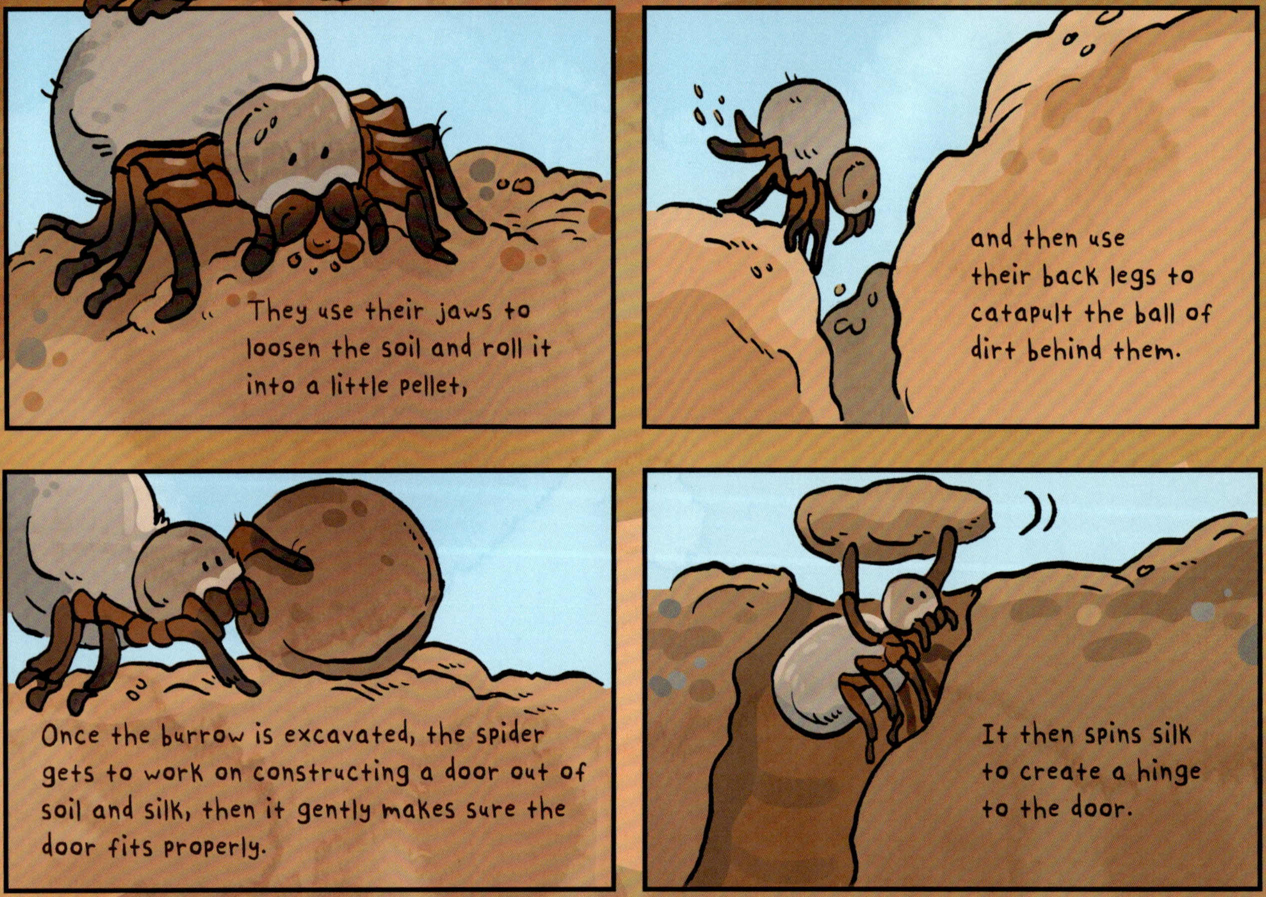
They use their jaws to loosen the soil and roll it into a little pellet,
and then use their back legs to catapult the ball of dirt behind them.
Once the burrow is excavated, the spider gets to work on constructing a door out of soil and silk, then it gently makes sure the door fits properly.
It then spins silk to create a hinge to the door.

When vibrations of walking feet set off the trap, the spider springs out of the door to strike!

POP GOES THE SPIDER!

These spiders can even eat animals as large as frogs and mice.

One specific type of trapdoor spider, called the cork-lid trapdoor spider, has an ornate butt. Their rear ends look like fancy sealing wax-stamped designs or some ancient coins!

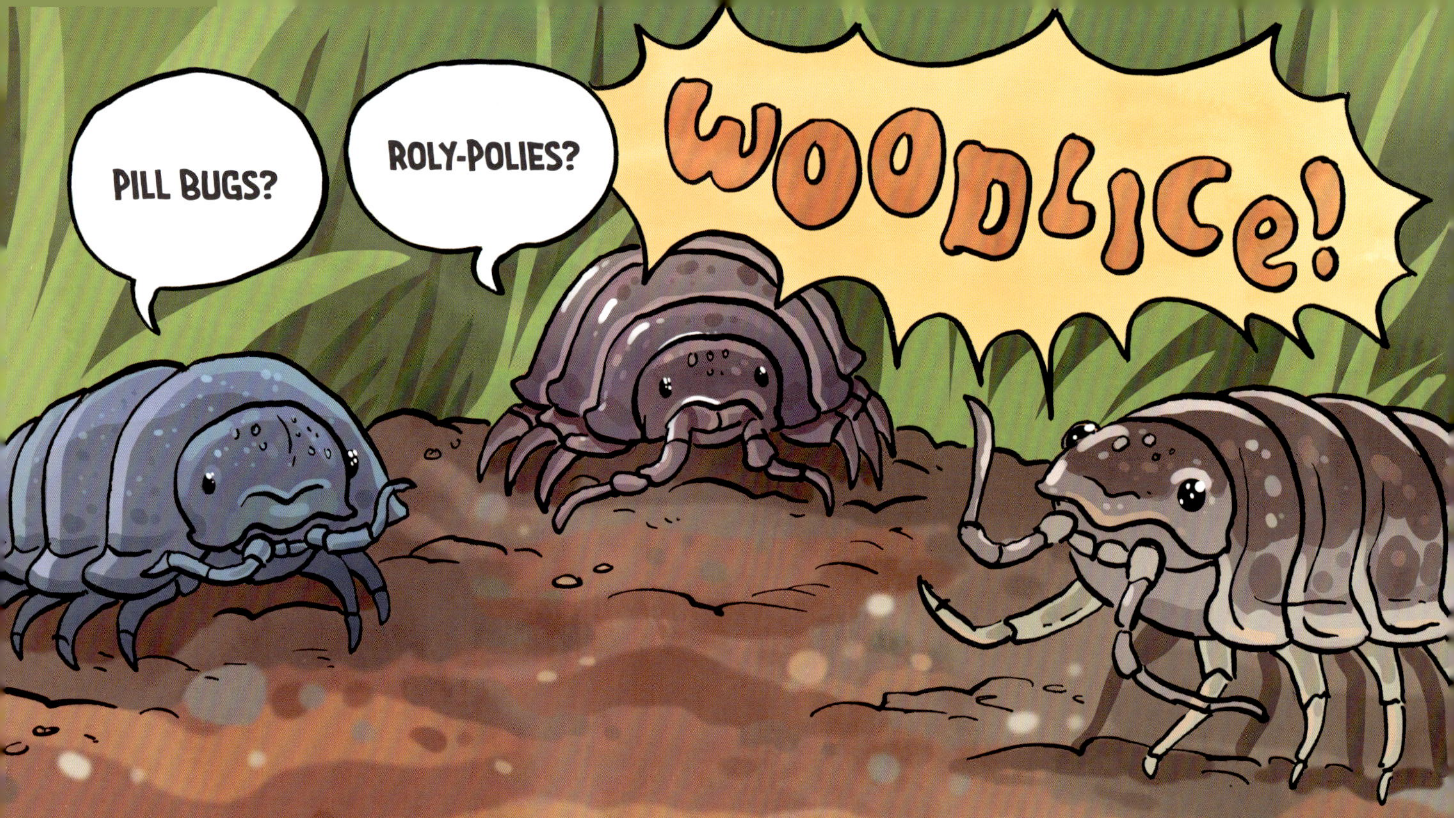
PILL BUGS?
ROLY-POLIES?
WOODLICE!

Woodlice are creatures with many names. In the United States, they're known as roly-polies, pill bugs, and doodle bugs. In the United Kingdom, they're known as chisel bobs, chuggie pigs, crunchy bats, Billy buttons...and the list goes on and on!

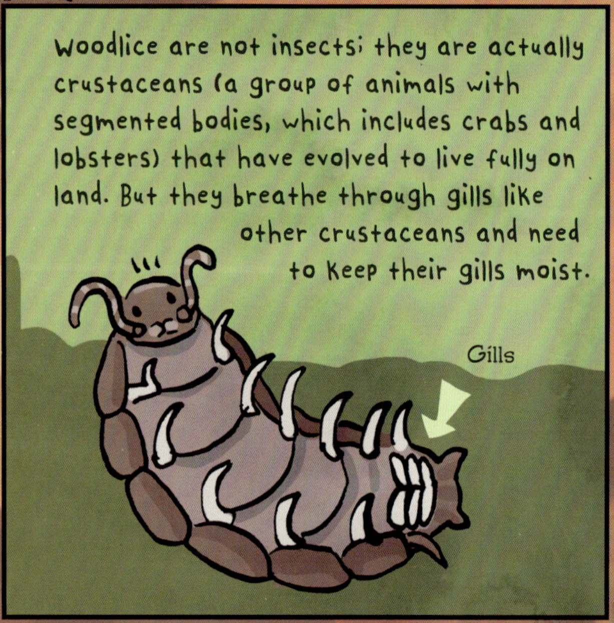
Woodlice are not insects; they are actually crustaceans (a group of animals with segmented bodies, which includes crabs and lobsters) that have evolved to live fully on land. But they breathe through gills like other crustaceans and need to keep their gills moist.
Gills

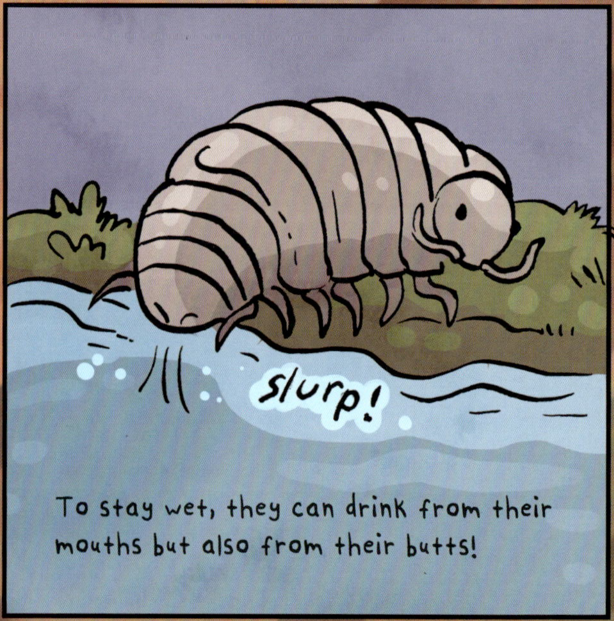
Slurp!
To stay wet, they can drink from their mouths but also from their butts!

MACROFAUNA

They are helpful soil decomposers and love to eat fallen leaves and other decomposing plant material. Woodlice are an important part of nutrient cycling.

They also eat their own poop, because their poop contains copper, which is essential to their diet.

ENJOY YOUR MEAL!

WASTE NOT, WANT NOT!

Mole Crickets' Sweet Serenade

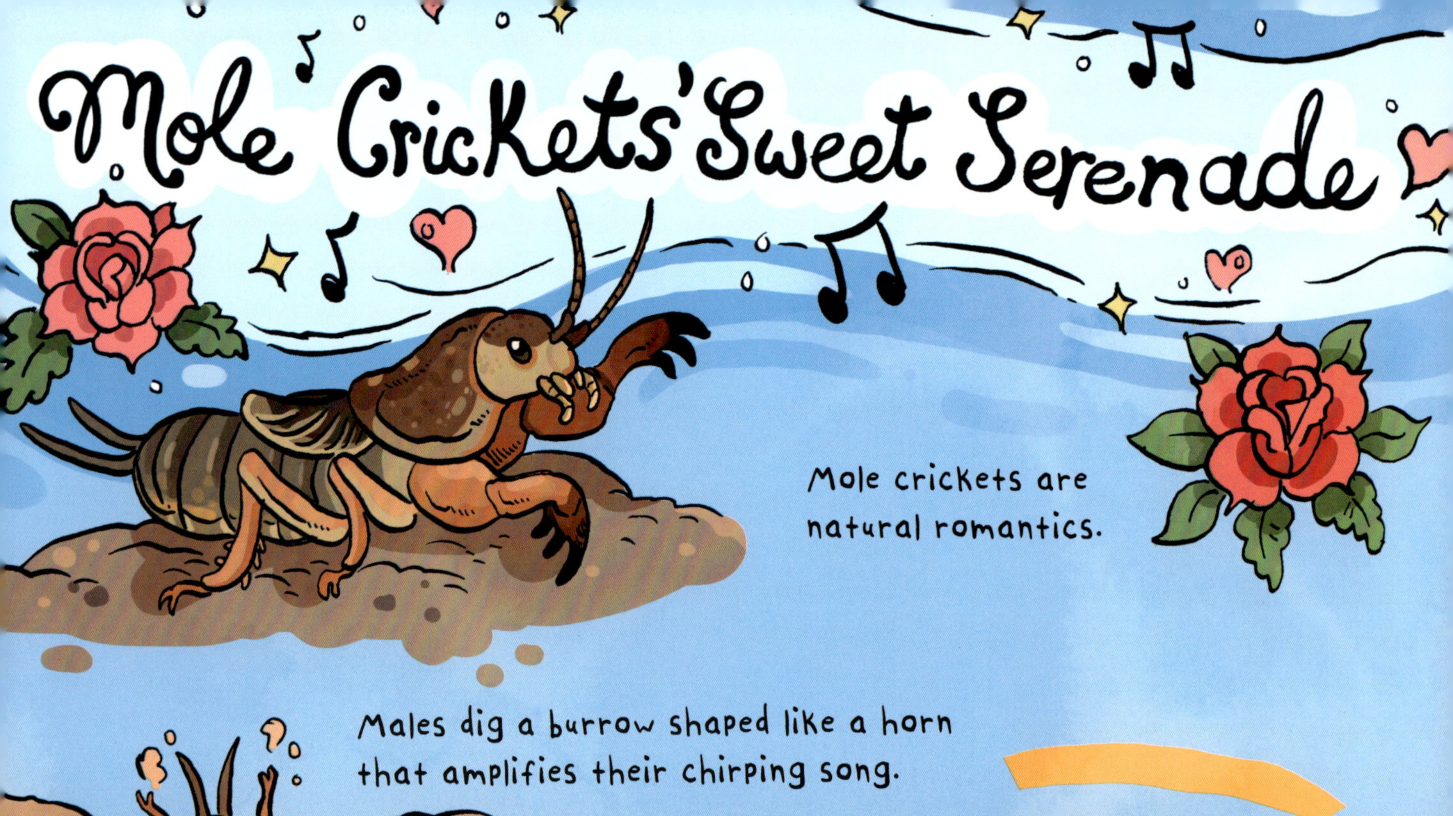

Mole crickets are natural romantics.

Males dig a burrow shaped like a horn that amplifies their chirping song.

Their song is LOUD, and as they are one of the loudest insects on earth, they can be heard over half a mile away.

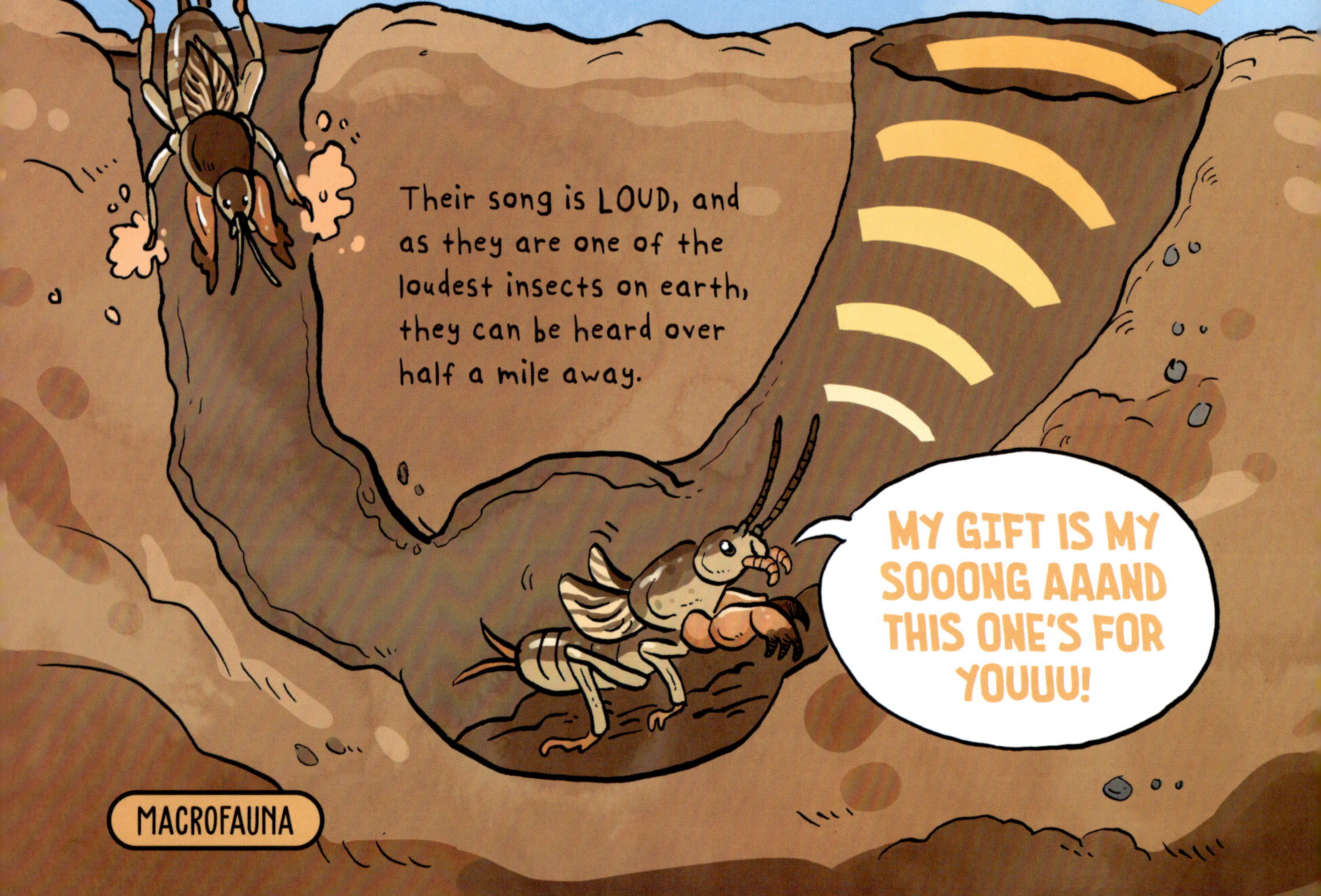
MY GIFT IS MY SOOONG AAAND THIS ONE'S FOR YOUUU!
MACROFAUNA

CHECK OUT THESE **SWEET DIGS!**

The male's song tells the female cricket where he can be found, but the sound also tells her about the structure of the burrow and the wetness of the soil, so she can tell if it is ideal for her eggs.

Mole crickets are designed for digging. They look like their namesake, the mole, with their large and powerful front legs.

They spend most of their time underground; some eat plant roots and others eat earthworms and small insects.

SEASON OF THE CICADAS

BUZZ, BUZZ, **BUUZZZZ!**

Annual

Periodical

Cicadas are known for their endless song in the summertime, but they spend most of their lives underground.

There are two main types of cicadas, periodical and annual cicadas. Annuals are usually larger and green, but periodical cicadas are black with red eyes. Annual cicadas emerge every year, but periodical cicadas emerge every thirteen or seventeen years!

Periodical cicadas have an especially interesting life cycle. Cicadas lay their eggs in trees, and when the eggs hatch...

Nymph

the nymph (juvenile) cicadas drop to the ground and burrow into the soil.

In the ground, they drink the sap of plant and tree roots.

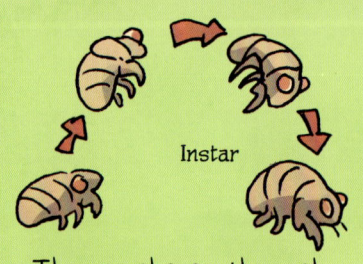

Instar

The nymphs go through different stages of growth called instars.

On their fifth instar stage, they emerge.

After seventeen long years, they dig themselves out of the soil and emerge from underground to find a mate.

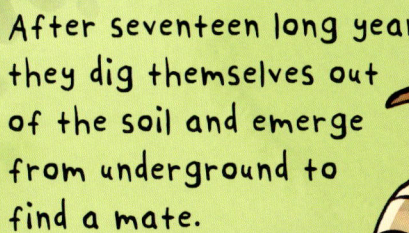

ZZZZ....YAAWNNN, WHAT A **GREAT** SEVENTEEN-YEAR NAP!

The nymphs climb up a tree, then molt (shed their old shell to grow larger) into their adult form.

Adult

Molt

They are white at first but turn a darker black color over time.

The male cicada will then sing his mating song, and if a female vibes with his sweet tunes, they'll mate and the female will produce eggs. The cycle will then begin all over again!

How do cicadas know when to dig themselves out? Scientists believe they sense through the changes in the tree sap they eat.

This internal clock keeps track of the tree changing and the passage of time. When the soil reaches a temperature of sixty-five degrees Fahrenheit, the cicadas know it's warm and time to emerge.

Rise of the Cicadas

Periodical cicadas come in broods, which are regional groups of cicadas that emerge at the same time. On very rare occasions, two broods from different regions can emerge at once, blanketing a huge area of the United States in singing cicadas!

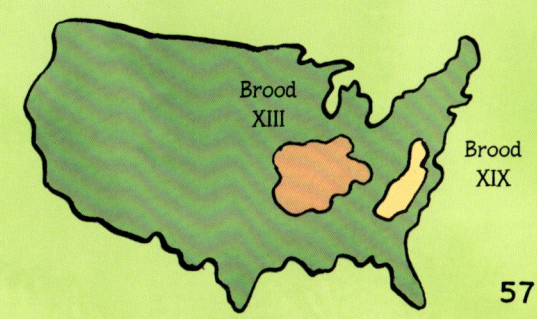

Brood XIII

Brood XIX

CICADA KILLER WASP ATTACK

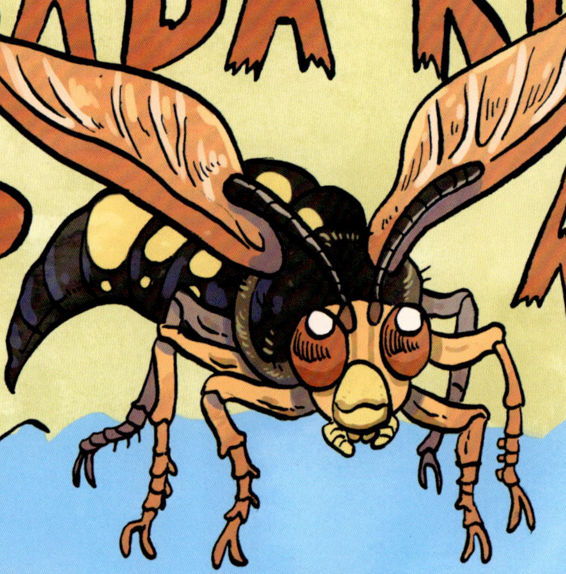

MACROFAUNA

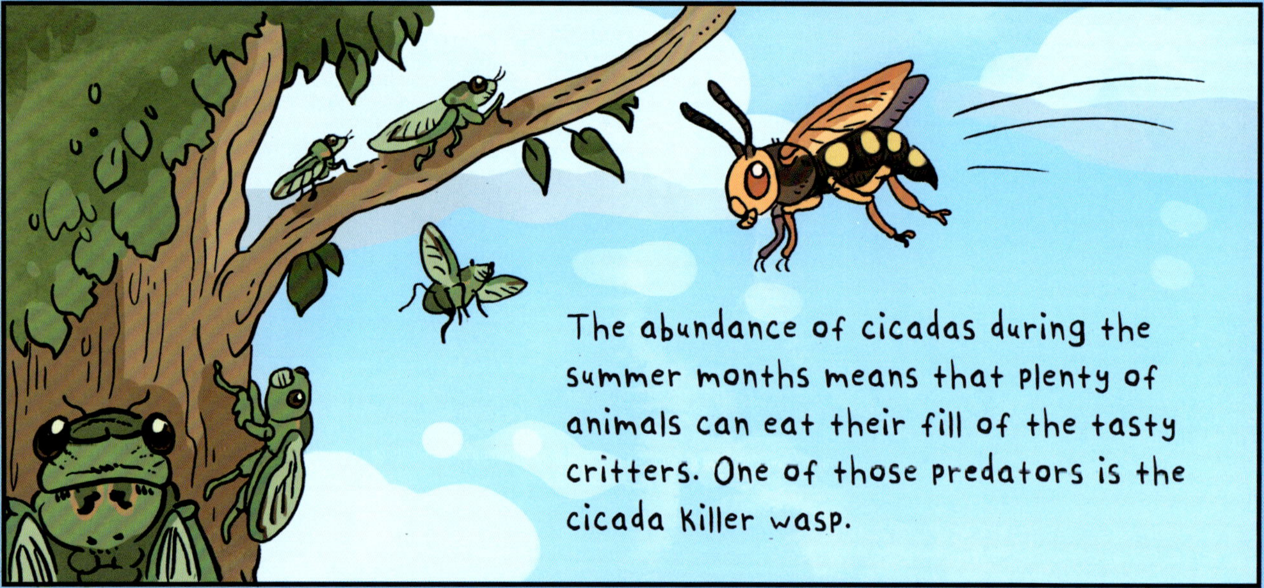
The abundance of cicadas during the summer months means that plenty of animals can eat their fill of the tasty critters. One of those predators is the cicada killer wasp.

These wasps are huge and often cause panic in humans because they have a painful sting. But they are only interested in hunting cicadas. And only the females can sting; the males can't sting at all.

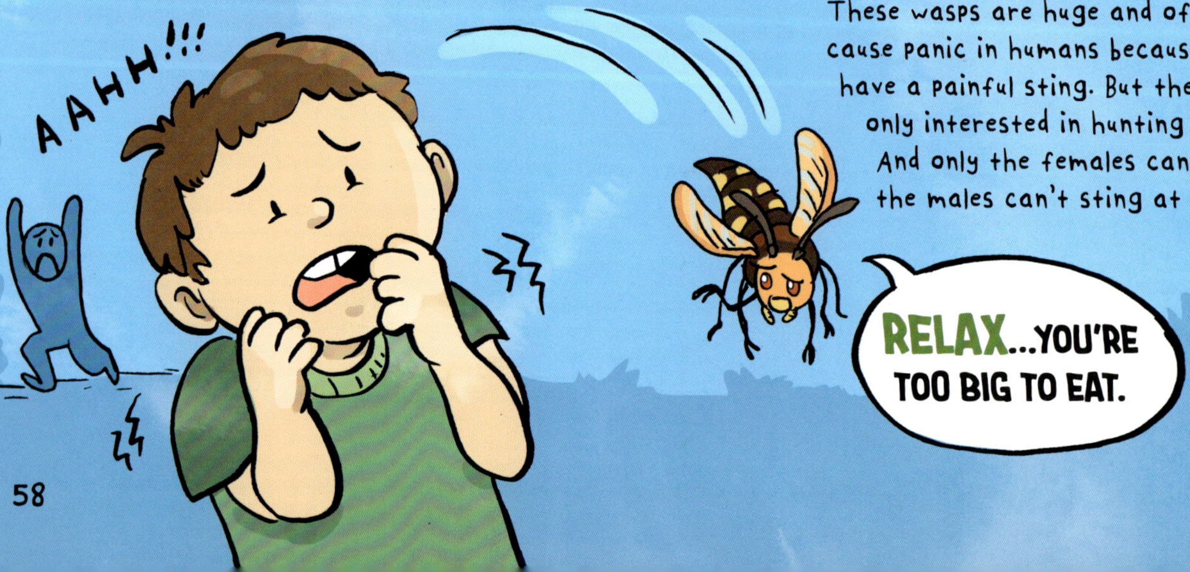
AAHH!!!
RELAX...YOU'RE TOO BIG TO EAT.

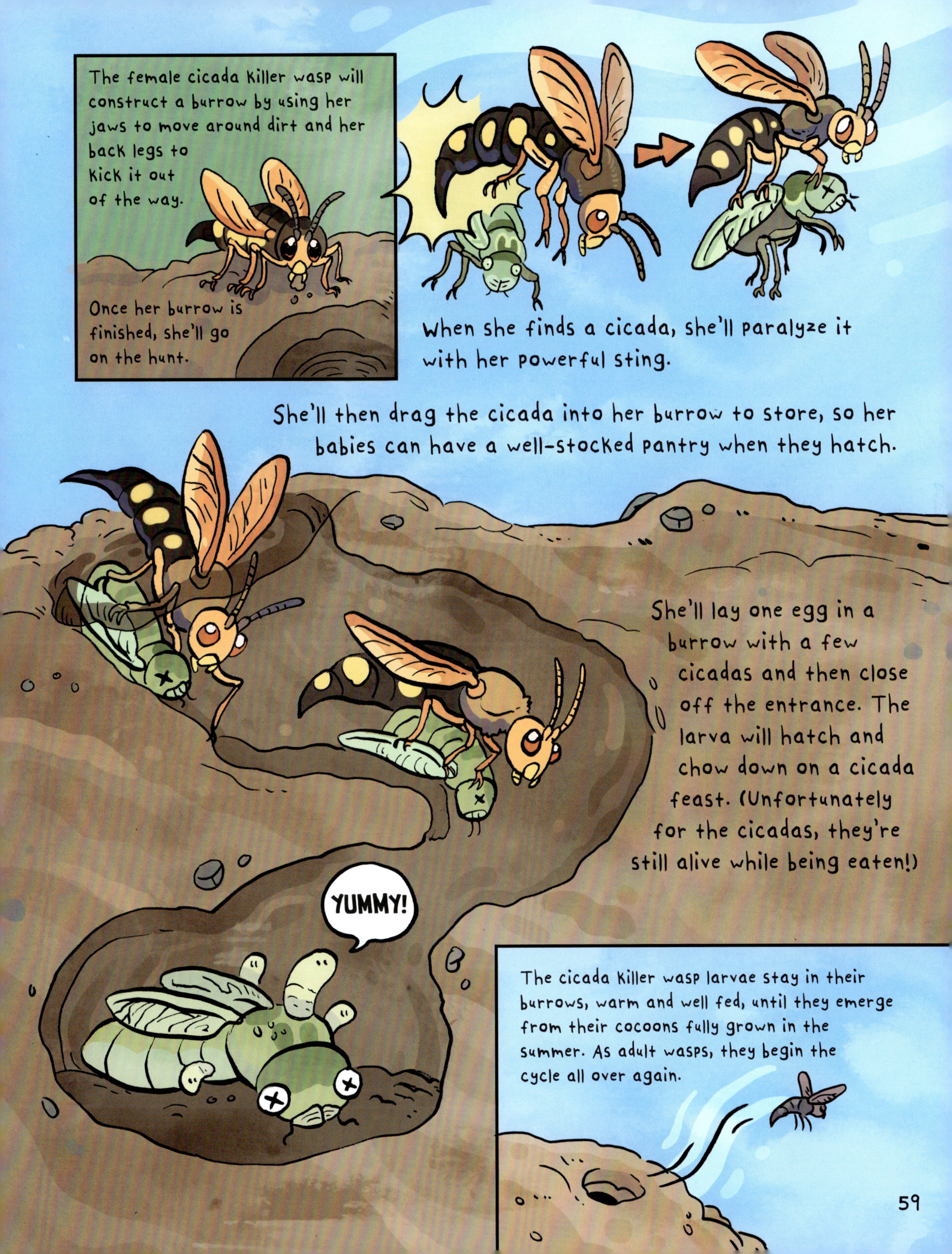
The female cicada killer wasp will construct a burrow by using her jaws to move around dirt and her back legs to kick it out of the way.
Once her burrow is finished, she'll go on the hunt.
When she finds a cicada, she'll paralyze it with her powerful sting.
She'll then drag the cicada into her burrow to store, so her babies can have a well-stocked pantry when they hatch.
She'll lay one egg in a burrow with a few cicadas and then close off the entrance. The larva will hatch and chow down on a cicada feast. (Unfortunately for the cicadas, they're still alive while being eaten!)
YUMMY!
The cicada killer wasp larvae stay in their burrows, warm and well fed, until they emerge from their cocoons fully grown in the summer. As adult wasps, they begin the cycle all over again.

Soil Beetles

MACROFAUNA

All dung beetles feed on poop and use it as their nests to lay their eggs, but different species of dung beetles have different approaches to making a home.

Dung Beetles

THIS POO IS MOVE-IN READY!

Some dung beetles called DWELLERS will just burrow into a fresh pile of poop as is and lay their eggs.

A TUNNEL IS THE PLACE FOR ME!

Others, called TUNNELERS, will dig a tunnel under the poop pile and slowly move bits of poop into their tunnels underground to lay eggs.

WE COULDN'T BE HAPPIER TO RELOCATE!

And the most well-known type of dung beetles, called ROLLERS, will grab a ball of poo away from the pile and roll it to a tunnel before they settle on a new location for their stinky home.

WE ARE VERY SELECTIVE.

ONLY THE FINEST FECES FOR ME, PLEASE!

Dung beetles can be very particular about poo. Many prefer to eat poop from herbivores (animals that eat only plants), which has a lot of plant matter. Others prefer omnivore (animals that eat both plants and other animals) poop, which is stinkier than other poop.

How do poop-rolling dung beetles navigate? By the stars!

During the day, dung beetles move in a straight line away from piles of poop by sensing light from the sun.

But at night, they find their way using the Milky Way and the stars.

Scientists that studied dung beetles realized that the beetles would roll in circles on cloudy nights, but on clear nights when the stars were visible, the beetles rolled their poop perfectly straight.

DEARLY BELOVED, WE ARE GATHERED HERE TODAY TO CELEBRATE THE LIFE OF THIS **TASTY MOUSE,** WHO WILL BECOME OUR DINNER.

American Burying Beetle

American burying beetles are nature's gravediggers and perform an important role of waste removal. They use their antennae to detect dead animals. Once a tasty dead animal is found, the beetles dig soil from under the animal, causing the corpse to sink beneath the dirt. They then perform a burial to hide it from other potential predators while covering it with secretions to protect the smell of the carcass from being discovered.

The female will work the carcass into the shape of a ball and lay her eggs in it, so the body will provide both a meal and a home to her children.

Acorn Weevils

Both male and female weevils have a long snout, called a rostrum, but females have longer rostrums to cut and drill into acorns that are still on the tree.

Rostrum

Once a hole is created, she will turn and lay an egg in the hole in the acorn, then plug up the hole again with poop.

MY BABIES WILL BE **SNUG AS A BUG** IN...AN ACORN!

Inside the acorns, the larvae eat away at the nut until autumn, when the acorn plummets from the branch onto the ground below. Then the larvae will chew open an escape hatch and squirm out of the acorn to burrow themselves deep into the soil.

In a few years, they will emerge from the soil to find a new acorn to lay eggs in, and the cycle starts again.

SOIL MEGAFAUNA: BIG Burrowers

Megafauna are larger animals—larger than earthworms—that live in underground burrows. Animals who are adapted to burrowing and living in the soil are called fossorial (fos-SOR-ree-uhl).

NOTHING BEATS BURROWING!

Star-Nosed Mole

Prairie Dog

Burrowing Owl

These animals can include mammals, birds, and reptiles. They often dig around so much that they loosen and aerate the soil. When soil is aerated, it becomes less tight and compact, so water and air can better move in between soil particles. Gardeners might be annoyed by their digging, but these animals contribute to the good physical condition of the soil, too.

Many burrowing animals provide a safe place for their families to live, but their burrows also serve as a home to other species of animals.

MAKE YOURSELVES AT HOME!

Gopher Tortoise

Welcome to Prairie Dog Town

MEGAFAUNA

The expansive and idyllic place called the Great Plains, which stretches from Canada to Mexico, is home to hundreds of black-tailed prairie dog families that live in spacious burrows underground.

One family group usually contains twelve individual dogs (one adult male, multiple adult females, and their young).

These prairie dogs live in a complex social family structure.

Close family groups in prairie dog towns will greet one another with a loving sniff and kiss.

Prairie dog towns even come with a sophisticated alarm system for the comfort and safety of all residents.

When a predator comes into view, lookouts will screech out a series of barks to warn all prairie dogs in the vicinity to dive into their tunnels.

Prairie dog towns used to dominate the landscape of the Great Plains of the United States...

but when ranchers arrived in the late 1800s, they set out to destroy them (mainly with poison).

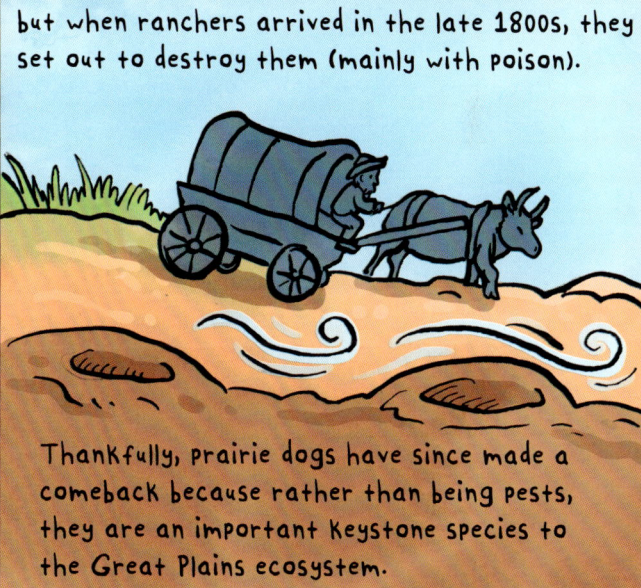

Thankfully, prairie dogs have since made a comeback because rather than being pests, they are an important keystone species to the Great Plains ecosystem.

Being a keystone species means they are very important to the environment around them because many other animals depend on them.

Animals such as badgers, bobcats, and the elusive black-footed ferret all eat prairie dogs, and they wouldn't be able to survive without them.

REMAIN CALM...

The STEALTHY Black-footed Ferret

MEGAFAUNA

Black-footed ferrets can't survive without prairie dogs because they're the ferrets' main source of food.

This adorable animal is really a skilled hunter with a powerful bite.

They're nocturnal, meaning they're active at night, and under the cover of darkness, they slip into prairie dog nests, sidling up to sleeping prairie dogs and biting them on the neck before they have a chance to escape.

Even though black-footed ferrets are small, they're voracious predators. One black-footed ferret can eat up to one hundred prairie dogs in a single year!

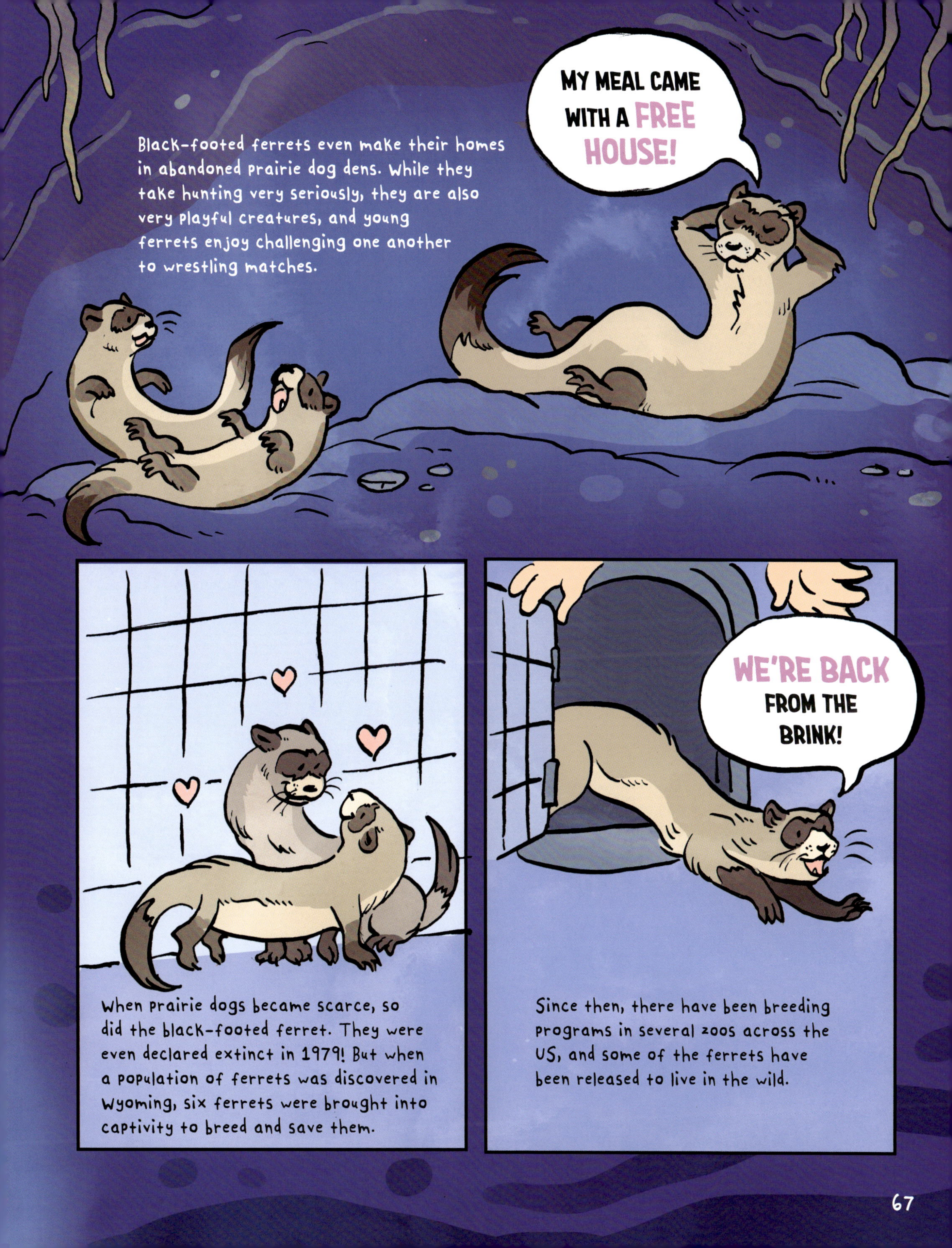
Black-footed ferrets even make their homes in abandoned prairie dog dens. While they take hunting very seriously, they are also very playful creatures, and young ferrets enjoy challenging one another to wrestling matches.
MY MEAL CAME WITH A FREE HOUSE!
When prairie dogs became scarce, so did the black-footed ferret. They were even declared extinct in 1979! But when a population of ferrets was discovered in Wyoming, six ferrets were brought into captivity to breed and save them.
WE'RE BACK FROM THE BRINK!
Since then, there have been breeding programs in several zoos across the US, and some of the ferrets have been released to live in the wild.

Home for a Burrowing Owl

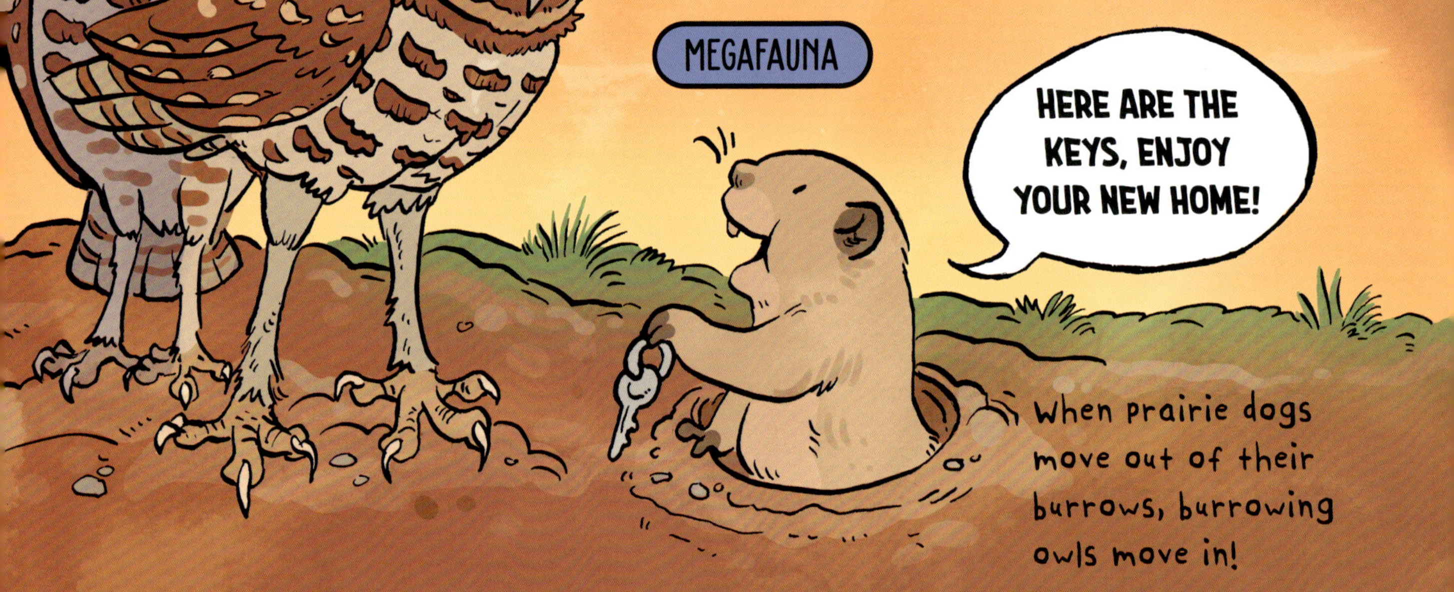
MEGAFAUNA
HERE ARE THE KEYS, ENJOY YOUR NEW HOME!

When prairie dogs move out of their burrows, burrowing owls move in!

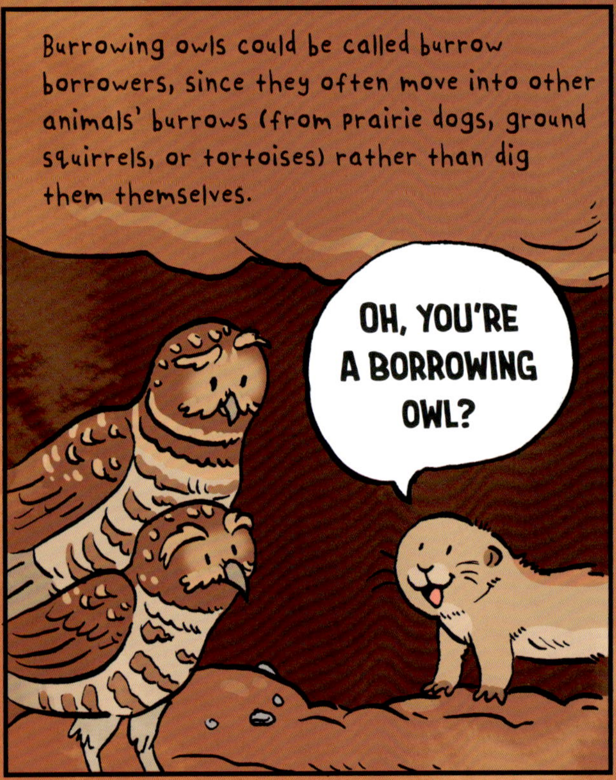
Burrowing owls could be called burrow borrowers, since they often move into other animals' burrows (from prairie dogs, ground squirrels, or tortoises) rather than dig them themselves.
OH, YOU'RE A BORROWING OWL?

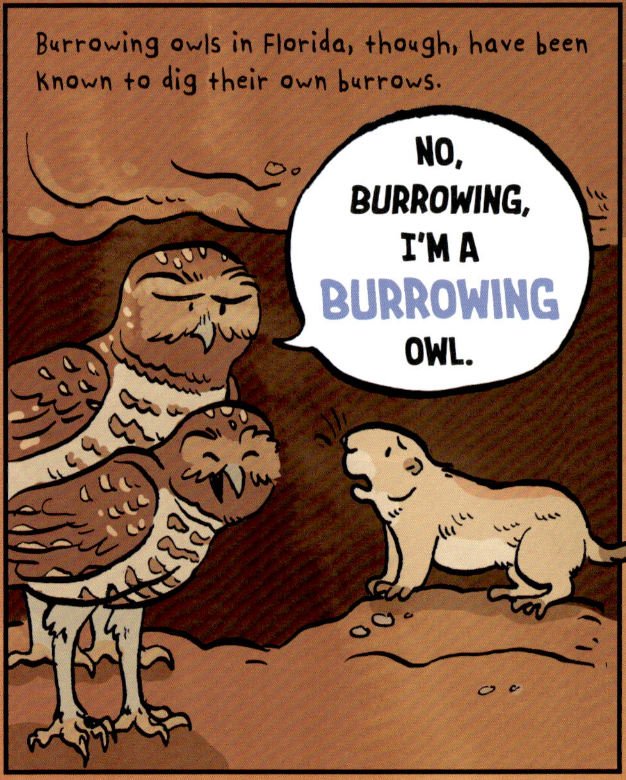
Burrowing owls in Florida, though, have been known to dig their own burrows.
NO, BURROWING, I'M A BURROWING OWL.

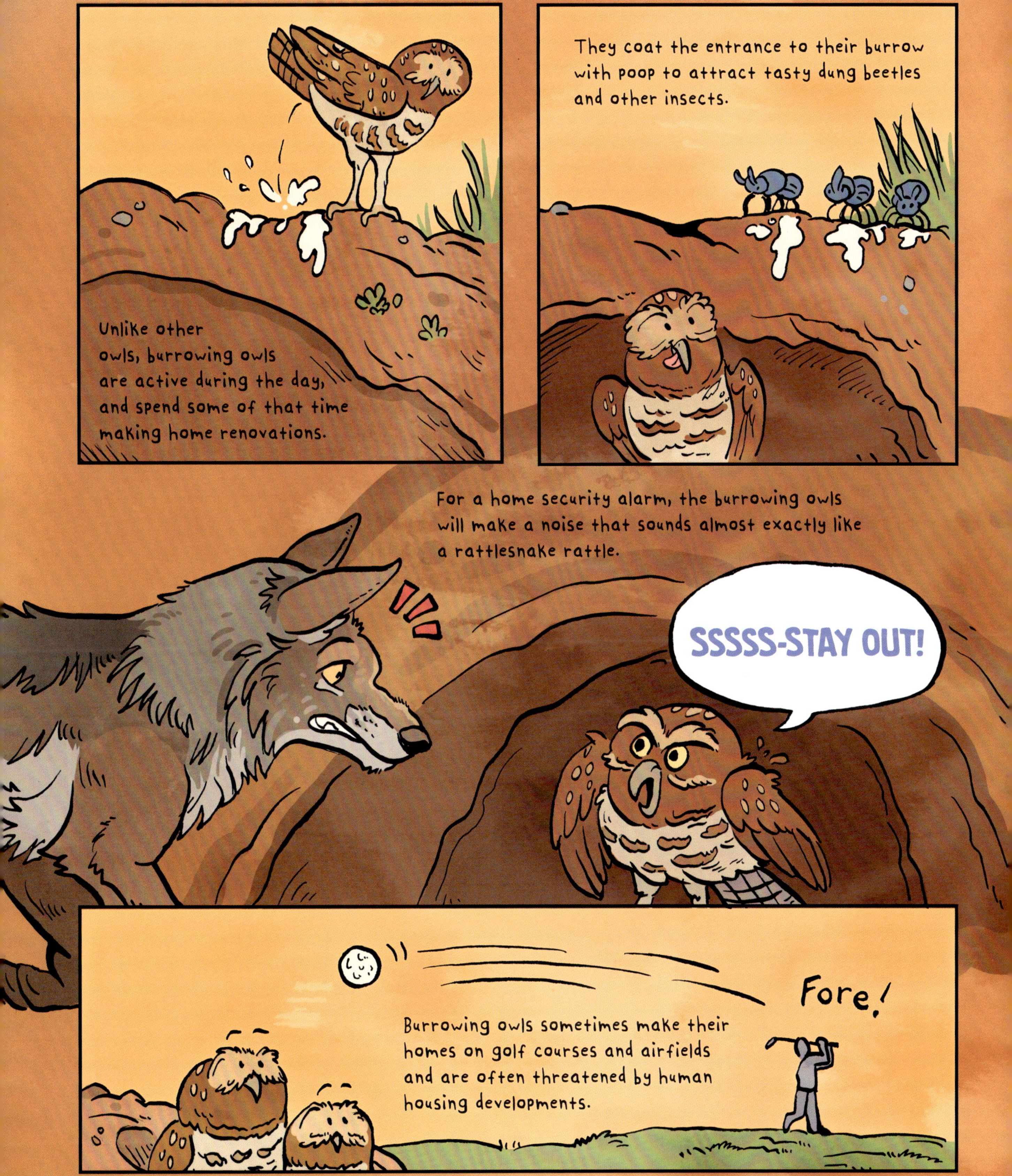
Unlike other owls, burrowing owls are active during the day, and spend some of that time making home renovations.
They coat the entrance to their burrow with poop to attract tasty dung beetles and other insects.
For a home security alarm, the burrowing owls will make a noise that sounds almost exactly like a rattlesnake rattle.
SSSSS-STAY OUT!
Fore!
Burrowing owls sometimes make their homes on golf courses and airfields and are often threatened by human housing developments.

Magnificent MOLES

European Mole

Some might consider a mole to be nothing more than a garden nuisance, but there is much more than meets the eye when it comes to these endearing and hardworking animals. They construct vast tunnel networks and can move 540 times their own body weight in dirt per day! Their fur is smooth and soft, and it helps them slide through the dirt easily.

They are true earthworm connoisseurs. Moles need to eat half of their weight in worms every day! Because earthworms are awfully gritty, moles squeeze them like a toothpaste tube to get all that icky dirt out of their meal before they eat the worms.

MEGAFAUNA

Star-Nosed Mole

These wriggling pink tentacles are not the limbs of a monstrous alien beast but, in fact, the nose of a type of mole. The star-nosed mole's snout is super sensitive. Not only is it an expert tunneler,, the star-nosed mole also knows how to swim!

Splash!

In fact, it lives much of its life in muddy burrows and swimming around looking for its prey of aquatic insects, small amphibians, and fish. While in the water, the star-nosed mole uses its nose to blow bubbles. It then snorts the bubbles back up so that it can smell underwater!

IT SMELLS... WET.

Golden Mole

The golden mole doesn't dig through gardens but instead the sandy soils of southern Africa. They can practically swim through the sand, but their movements don't leave tunnels behind.

WHERE IS IT??

These disappearing trails can make them difficult to find, and in 2023, a species of golden mole called De Winton's golden mole was rediscovered after being unseen for almost ninety years!

OVER HERE!

Golden moles can grow up to nine inches long. They get all the liquid they need from the food they eat (small insects, lizards, and snakes), so they don't need to drink. They are not actually true moles and are more closely related to aardvarks than they are to other mole species.

THE INDESTRUCTIBLE NAKED MOLE RAT

MEGAFAUNA

Some might say that with their beady little eyes and wrinkled nude skin, naked mole rats aren't the most pleasant animals to look at.

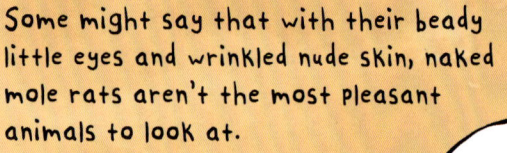

HEY, LOOKS **AREN'T** EVERYTHING!

Their odd looks serve a purpose. Their baggy, saggy skin doesn't tear if they get stuck on something while they are digging.

Their teeth are in front of their lips so dirt doesn't get in their mouths while they are arranging themselves neatly in an assembly line to excavate the soil.

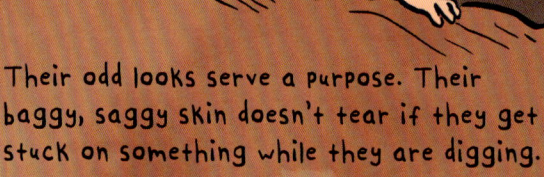

CHOMP

Naked mole rats are unlike any other mammal because they are eusocial like ants and termites. They live in an underground colony with a queen and workers.

MY LIEGE...

So, who can get crowned as the naked mole rat queen?

VS

Females fight for the position, and it can be brutal!

Once a mole rat becomes queen, her body changes and elongates to fit more babies inside it.

If that wasn't interesting enough, naked mole rats have many unusual powers. They can live a long time—up to thirty years. They are also resistant to cancer. They don't feel much pain, and they hardly show signs of aging.

THE HEROIC GOPHER TORTOISE

The gopher tortoise is a true superhero! It is known as a keystone species, which means that many other animals depend on this unassuming creature.

Gopher tortoises are only about a foot long, but they dig deep tunnels (up to forty feet long!), which many other animals will move into to cool down and escape the summer heat.

The tortoise won't even mind if other creatures, such as rattlesnakes, burrowing owls, and eastern cottontail rabbits, hang out with them in the tunnels.

FEEL FREE TO STOP BY ANYTIME!

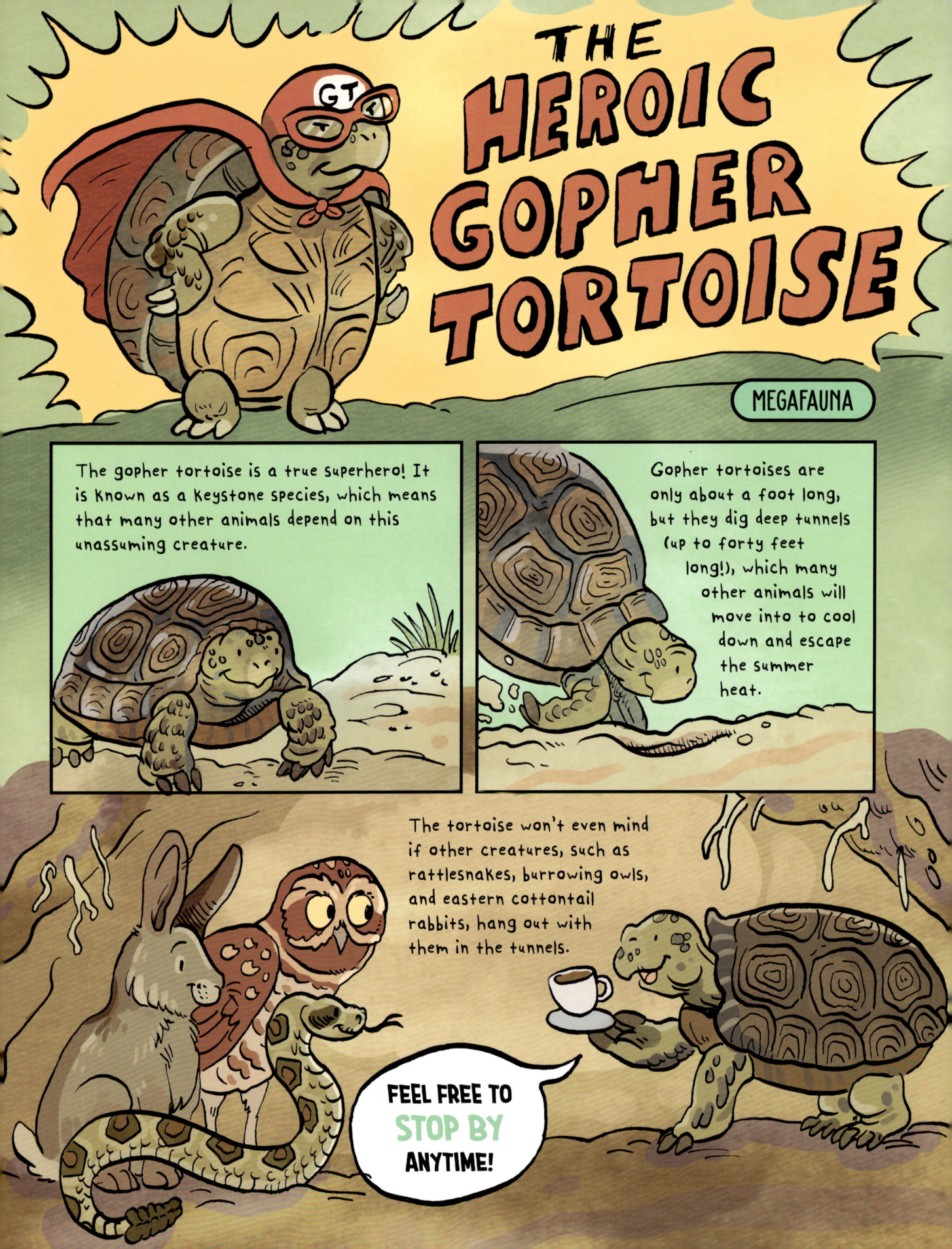

Most importantly, gopher tortoise burrows can become a lifesaving refuge for animals escaping the flames of a brush fire. In the pine forest environment of Florida, fire is revitalizing to the habitat because the older pine trees can withstand the blaze and the fire will clear out other scrub, allowing new pine trees to grow. But when a fire breaks out, the animals on the ground are at risk if they don't find somewhere to hide.

Birds can fly away, fish are safe in the water, but ground-dwelling animals need to find an escape FAST. So they scurry to gopher tortoise burrows to stay safe and sound underground.

Phew!

In this way, the tortoise deserves a medal and a front-page feature in the *Pine Forest Gazette*.

LOCAL HERO TORTOISE SAVES US ALL!

YOU'RE OUR HERO!

The Marvelous Meerkat

Meerkats live in tightly knit family groups of anywhere from three to twenty-five members. A group of meerkats is known as a mob.

DON'T MESS WITH MEERKATS!

MEGAFAUNA

They band together to appear larger and scare away any predators. The black markings around their faces protect their eyes from the sun, like sunglasses.

Mobs roam African grasslands, looking for one of their favorite foods: scorpions. They are immune to the scorpion's sting and simply bite off the stingers and then chow down on these crunchy treats. Other than scorpions, they eat everything from reptiles to birds to fruits.

CHOMP

Just like prairie dogs, meerkats live in social groups in underground burrows to avoid the hot sun.

They dig their burrows using their sharp claws. Sentries alert the mob to danger with a high-pitched call, and devoted babysitters care for pups.

TIME TO BRUSH YOUR TEETH AND GET READY FOR BED!

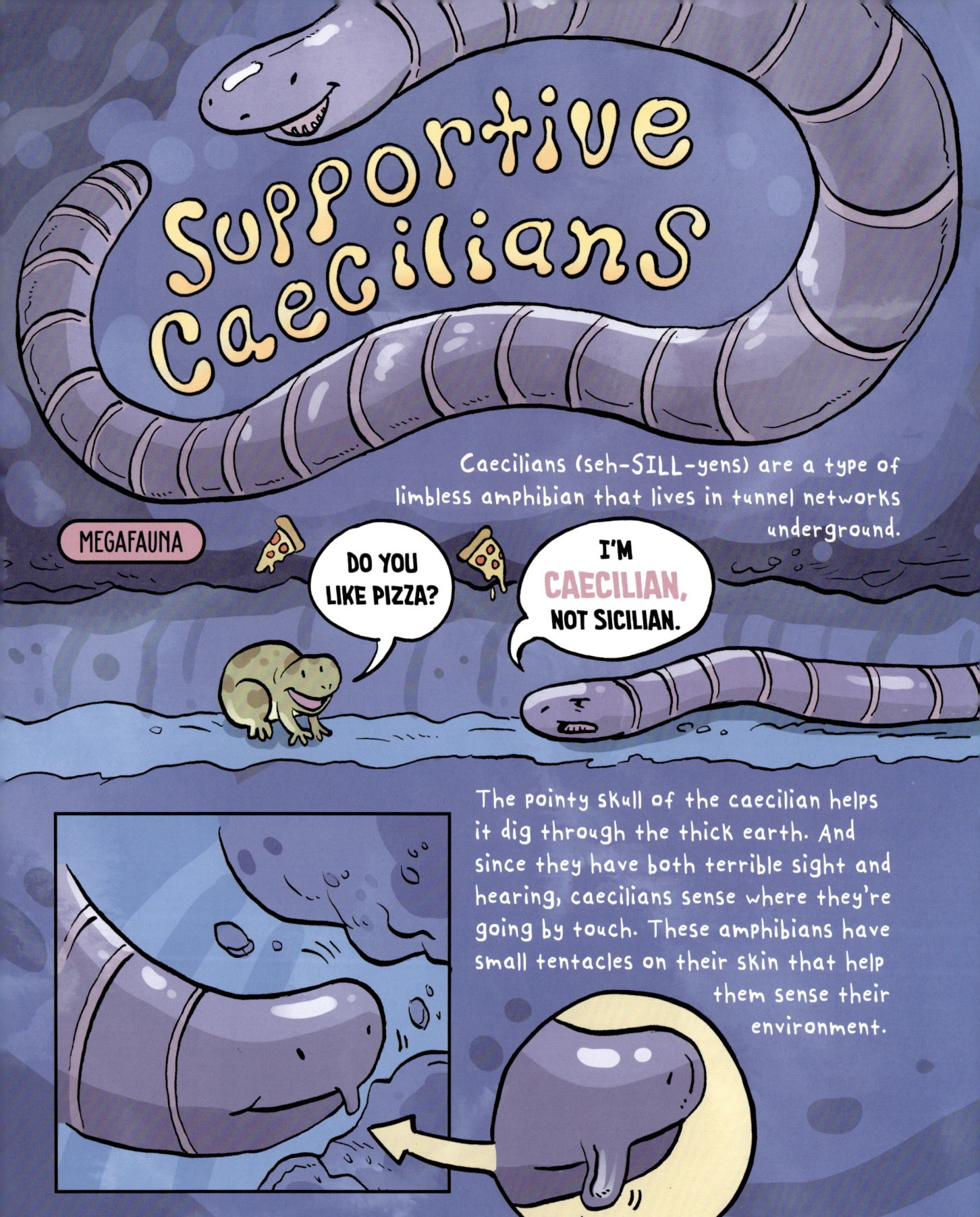

Supportive Caecilians

Caecilians (seh-SILL-yens) are a type of limbless amphibian that lives in tunnel networks underground.

MEGAFAUNA

DO YOU LIKE PIZZA?

I'M CAECILIAN, NOT SICILIAN.

The pointy skull of the caecilian helps it dig through the thick earth. And since they have both terrible sight and hearing, caecilians sense where they're going by touch. These amphibians have small tentacles on their skin that help them sense their environment.

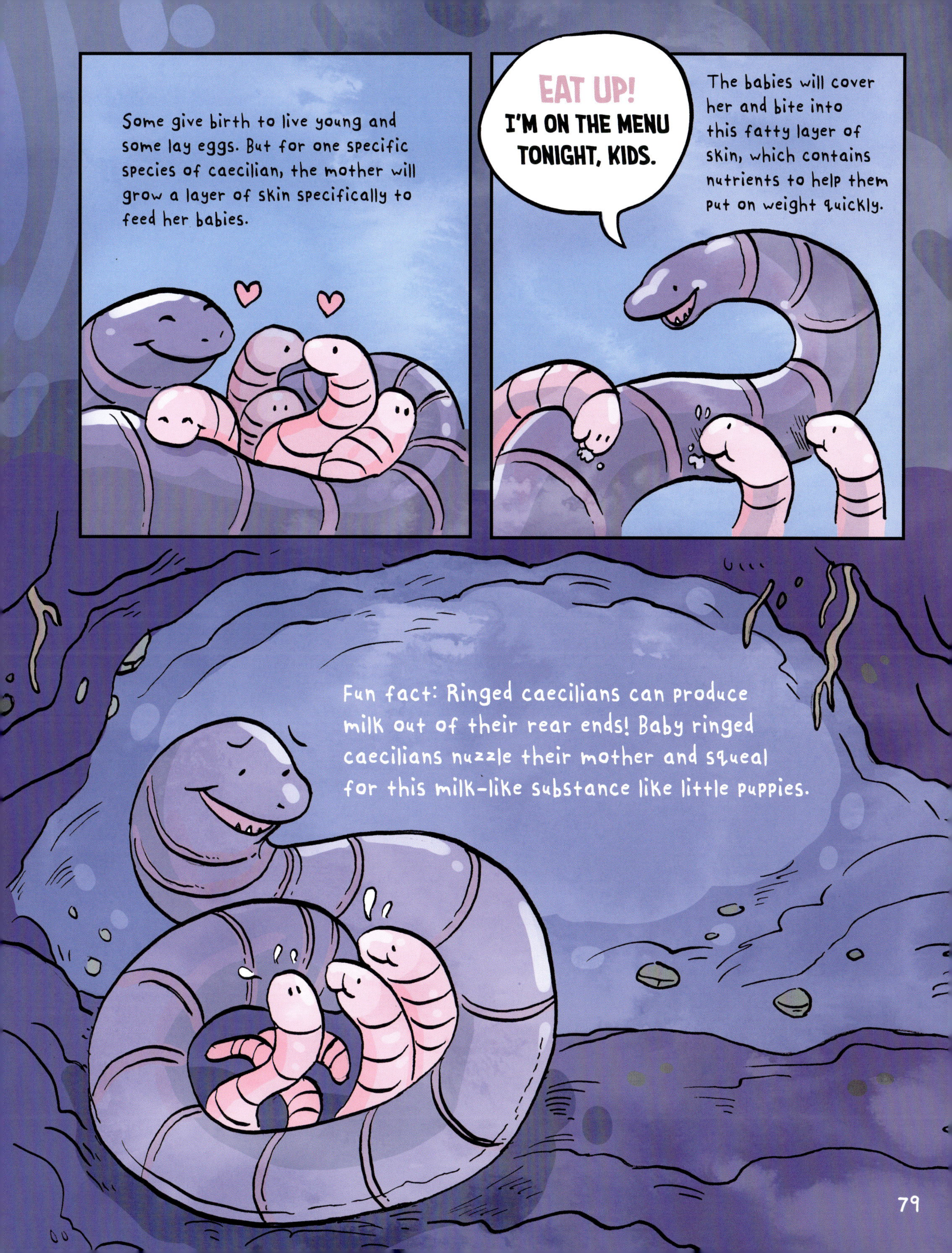
Some give birth to live young and some lay eggs. But for one specific species of caecilian, the mother will grow a layer of skin specifically to feed her babies.
EAT UP! I'M ON THE MENU TONIGHT, KIDS.
The babies will cover her and bite into this fatty layer of skin, which contains nutrients to help them put on weight quickly.
Fun fact: Ringed caecilians can produce milk out of their rear ends! Baby ringed caecilians nuzzle their mother and squeal for this milk-like substance like little puppies.

MEXICAN MOLE LIZARD

MEGAFAUNA

Mole lizards are a type of lizard called an amphisbaena (am-fis-BAY-nah), named after the mythical two-headed snake of the same name. But instead of two heads, these lizards have two small legs, each with five toes, which help them to burrow.

The mole lizard is between seven and nine inches long and lives on the Baja California peninsula in Mexico.

They're bright pink, and like the caecilians, they burrow through the soil with their heads (as well as their little legs). Mexican mole lizards are only about the size of an earthworm, but they also eat earthworms themselves, as well as termites and cockroach eggs.

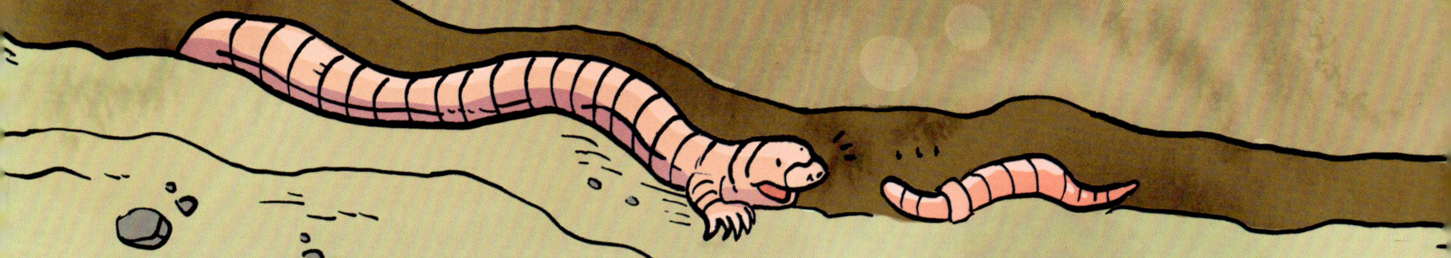

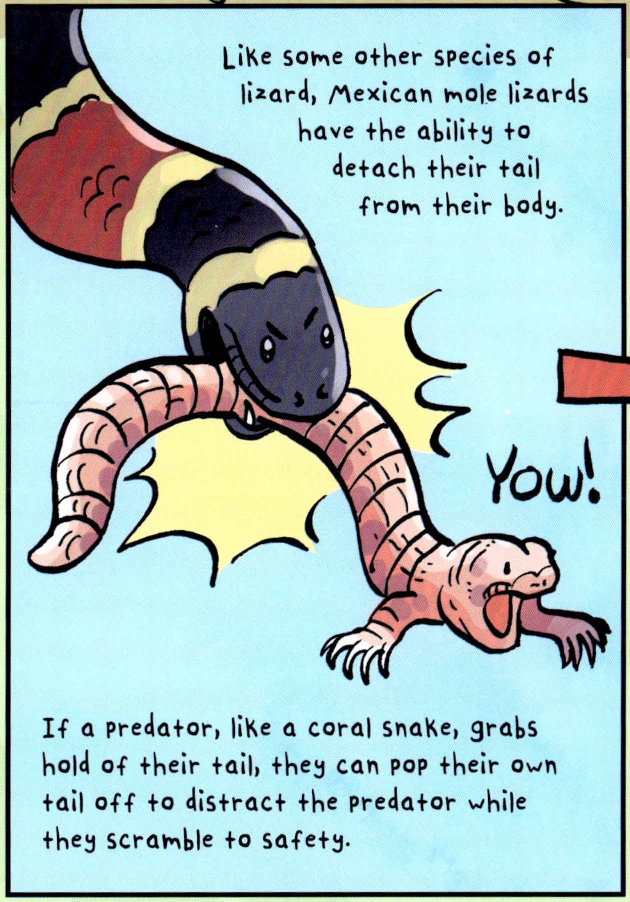

Like some other species of lizard, Mexican mole lizards have the ability to detach their tail from their body.
YOW!
If a predator, like a coral snake, grabs hold of their tail, they can pop their own tail off to distract the predator while they scramble to safety.

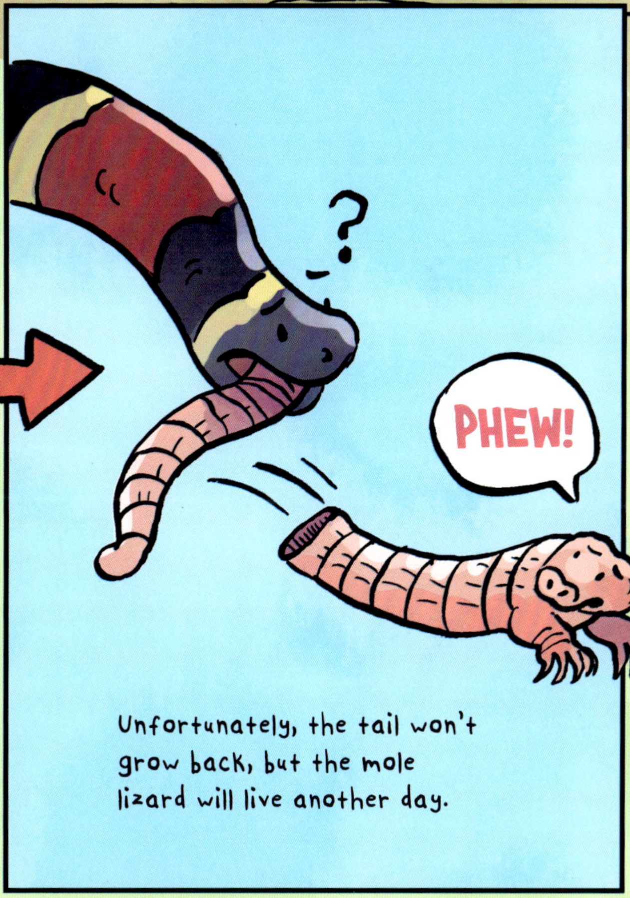

?
PHEW!
Unfortunately, the tail won't grow back, but the mole lizard will live another day.

Toilet Trouble

There's a sinister urban legend about the innocent mole lizard. The myth says that they like to lurk in toilets, wait until an unsuspecting person sits down, and crawl up their rear end! But that is far from the truth; they prefer their underground desert habitat to a toilet bowl.

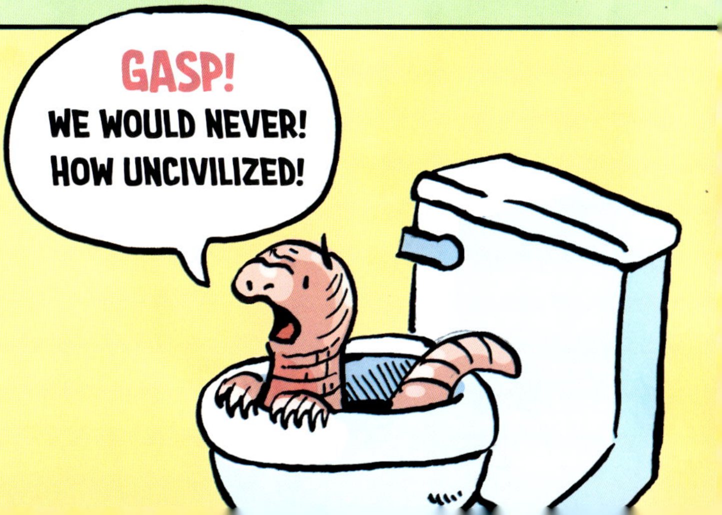

GASP!
WE WOULD NEVER! HOW UNCIVILIZED!

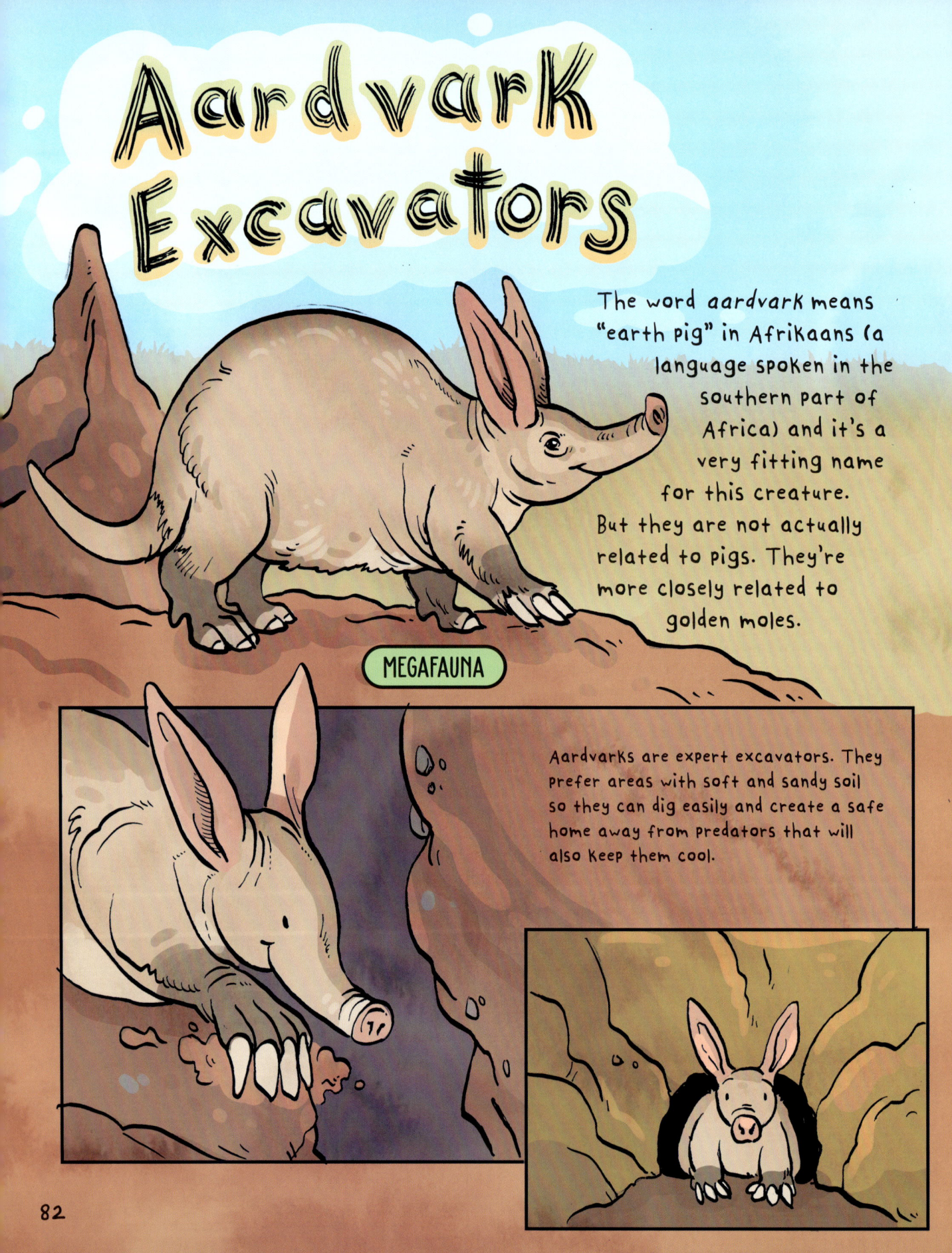

Aardvark Excavators

The word *aardvark* means "earth pig" in Afrikaans (a language spoken in the southern part of Africa) and it's a very fitting name for this creature. But they are not actually related to pigs. They're more closely related to golden moles.

MEGAFAUNA

Aardvarks are expert excavators. They prefer areas with soft and sandy soil so they can dig easily and create a safe home away from predators that will also keep them cool.

Their burrows have multiple rooms. Like with gopher tortoises and prairie dogs, many other animals move into the burrows that aardvarks create. Aardvarks are known for eating ants and termites, and it's true their diets mostly consist of those pint-size architects. But...

Warthog

Bat-Eared Foxes

African Crested Porcupine

WE ALSO LOVE CUCUMBERS. I'M NOT KIDDING!

The aardvark cucumber is a plant that has developed a close relationship with its namesake animal. It's the only fruit they will eat.

An aardvark will eat a cucumber, and then poop out the seeds. The cucumber seeds sprout and grow especially well in the rich aardvark poop.

Anteater? Aardvark? What's the difference?

These animals are often confused for each other. They do have similarities, but they are completely different species. Aardvarks live in sub-Saharan Africa, and anteaters live in South America. Giant anteaters are much furrier than aardvarks, and aardvarks have much longer ears than anteaters. But both animals love eating ants and termites, and they both use their sharp claws to dig out ant and termite nests.

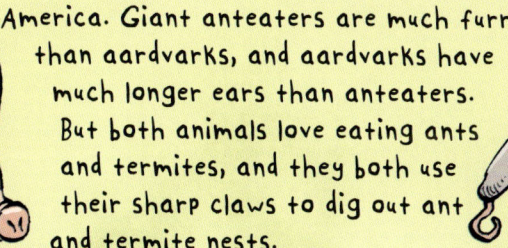

ARMADILLO ARMY

In Spanish, *armadillo* means "little armored one." There are many different types of armadillos, and they are found primarily in Mexico, South America, and the southern United States.

There were once giant armadillos called glyptodonts, which were dinosaur-size armadillos that lived thousands of years ago. Ancient humans even hunted them for food!

The tunnels that these massive animals dug can still be found. They are so big, humans can stand up in them!

MEGAFAUNA

Nine-Banded Armadillo

The nine-banded armadillo is perhaps the most well-known armadillo, with a long snout, large ears, and the bands that create its hard shell (and despite its name, the number of bands ranges from seven to eleven). It is the only armadillo species that is found in the United States. Contrary to popular belief, nine-banded armadillos cannot curl completely up into a ball (only three-banded armadillos can do that!).

Speech bubble: DO YOU BELIEVE IN **FAIRIES?**

Pink Fairy Armadillo

The adorable pink fairy armadillo is the world's smallest armadillo at only about six inches long. The pink fairy armadillo can control the blood vessels in its shell to regulate its body temperature. Because they spend most of their lives underground, they are difficult to study and little is known about them.

Speech bubble: **AAAAAAHHH!** THEY DON'T CALL ME THE **SCREAMING HAIRY ARMADILLO** FOR NOTHING!

Screaming Hairy Armadillo

When threatened by a predator, the screaming hairy armadillo lets out a bloodcurdling shriek! They have a thick armor made of about eighteen bands, and their bodies are covered in boney plates with overlapping scales called scutes. Their hair grows out from between the scutes all around their bodies, and they are hairier than other species of armadillos.

Giant Armadillo

The giant armadillo dwarfs the pink fairy armadillo as the world's largest armadillo (that is not extinct). It can weigh up to 150 pounds! Its huge middle front claws can be eight inches long and are the largest claws of any living animal.

Burrowers Down Under

MEGAFAUNA

Because the landmass of Australia has been isolated from the rest of the world for thirty-five million years, there's no shortage of strange animals that have evolved there. And the echidna, wombat, and bilby are no exception. They are all mammals, but echidnas are monotremes, a special group of egg-laying mammals (which also includes the platypus).

Echidna

Echidnas have backward-facing hind feet! It's hard to tell if they're coming or going based on their footprints. These strangely oriented feet help them dig faster and more efficiently. If a predator comes along, an echidna will burrow into the soil quickly with only their quills poking out to stop any predators in their tracks.

Wombat

Wombats are strong diggers that can move a lot of dirt in a single night. They construct burrows to escape the harsh Australian heat and hide from predators like dingoes and foxes. Wombat tunnels are huge, big enough for a person to crawl into!

Fun fact: Wombats have square poop! But why? Scientists believe they evolved this way so that their poop won't roll away and can be left behind to better mark their territory. The square poop shape is created by the unique movements of the wombat's intestines.

HOW CONVENIENT!

Bilby

Bilbies look like a cross between a rat and a rabbit. They are expert diggers. Female bilbies even have backward pouches, so the dirt doesn't fill her pouch when she's digging!

Bunnies vs. Bilbies!

Bilbies are native to Australia, and they are unfortunately endangered. Rabbits are considered invasive pests in the country. Because of this, there has been a movement to replace the traditional Easter Bunny with an Easter Bilby, and chocolate bilbies can be found in stores as an alternative to chocolate bunnies.

HAPPY EASTER!

Groundhog Day!

Groundhogs, also known as woodchucks, are the largest member of the ground squirrel family. They are stocky animals and can weigh up to fourteen pounds. They can be found anywhere from Alaska to Canada and the eastern United States.

They live in underground burrows, where they have different chambers; a large chamber serves as a living room, while another chamber is used as a bathroom. Groundhogs are true hibernators, and over the long winter, they will curl into a ball, lower their body temperature, and slow their breathing and heart rate.

In this deep slumber, they will wake up a few times to go to the bathroom, but they won't need to eat anything until they wake up in the spring.

Fact or fiction?

Groundhog Day is celebrated on February 2 in Canada and the United States. If a groundhog comes out of its burrow on this day and sees its shadow, there will be six more weeks of winter.

Is there any scientific truth to the groundhog's weather predictions? The truth is we just don't know for sure.

Sensational Shrews

Shrews are not rodents (a group of animals that have continuously growing teeth that includes mice, rats, squirrels, and more). They are more closely related to moles. Many shrews are excellent burrowers and live most of their lives underground and out of sight.

Shrews need to consume a huge amount of food to stay alive, which means they need to eat more than their body weight in invertebrates, like insects, earthworms, and snails, every day.

MEGAFAUNA

Solenodon

The solenodon is a large shrewlike animal that can grow up to fifteen inches long. They're large enough to eat crabs, lizards, and snakes. Solenodons (along with certain types of shrews) are one of the only venomous mammals in the world. Their venom is similar to a viper's (a type of snake) and they are able to inject it with their bottom teeth.

Short-Eared Elephant Shrew

Short-eared elephant shrews prefer a sandy soil that they can burrow into. Elephant shrews are part of an order of animals called afrotherians, which includes golden moles, aardvarks, dugongs, and even elephants! But these shrews are nowhere near elephant size. In fact, they're only four inches long.

HOW'S THE WEATHER UP THERE?

Burrowing Badgers

Badgers are icons of the British countryside, but there are many other varieties of badger that exist all around the world. Badgers are part of a group called mustelids (MUST-ehl-id), which includes otters, weasels, wolverines, and ferrets.

MEGAFAUNA

They're stocky and powerful animals that are omnivorous (meaning they eat both plants and animals). Male badgers are called boars, and females are called sows.

European Badger (Europe)

These are very social animals who enjoy snuggling together in a heap. They live in family groups, and their home is called a sett. Badgers prefer a clean house; they won't bring any food into their home (no need to set the table in their sett!), and they won't even poo in their sett, instead using a nearby pit for their toilet. They dine on earthworms, berries, and insects.

American Badger (United States)

American badgers are solitary animals who love their alone time, but they have been observed palling around with coyotes and even hunting together. Coyotes easily chase down prey, while badgers can dig any fleeing creature out of its burrow. Hunting this way allows these animals to have a greater chance of catching a meal than either of them would have on their own.

Honey Badger (Africa, Western Asia)

Honey badgers are known for their fierce, tenacious personalities. When threatened, the honey badger will roar, release a stink bomb of foul-smelling liquid from a gland in their butt, much like a skunk, and charge at an enemy.

They often take over other animals' burrows, including those of cape foxes, bat-eared foxes, and yellow mongooses.

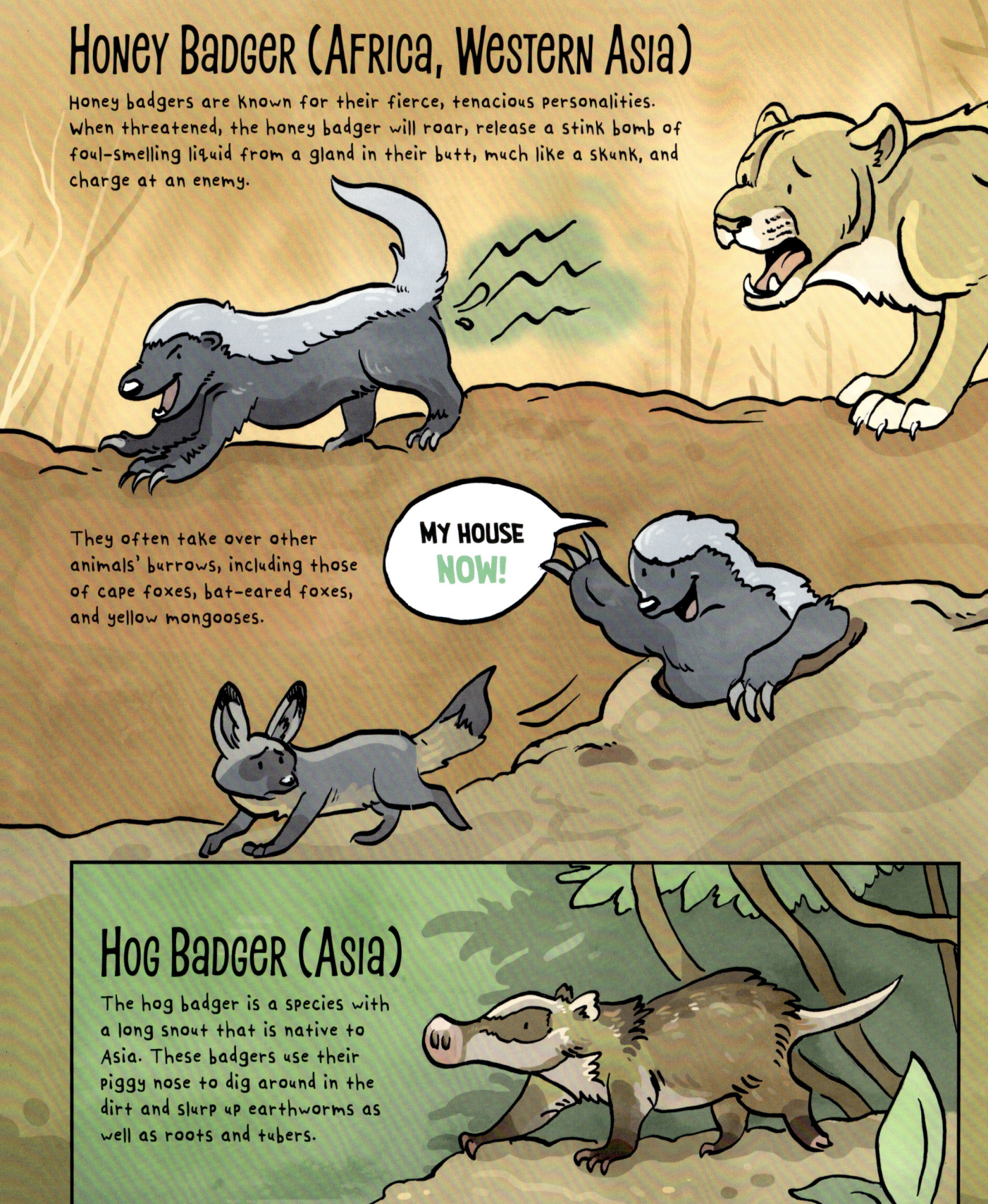

MY HOUSE NOW!

Hog Badger (Asia)

The hog badger is a species with a long snout that is native to Asia. These badgers use their piggy nose to dig around in the dirt and slurp up earthworms as well as roots and tubers.

Save the Soil!

Healthy soil is essential for the well-being of life on earth. The soil is both a precious resource for humans to grow food and a complex interconnected ecosystem full of the wonderful critters found in this book. Here are some threats to the soil community and ways we can overcome them.

EROSION

Topsoil

The thin layer of topsoil on our planet is essential to life. One inch of precious topsoil can take hundreds of years to form, as the soil is created when weather slowly wears down rocks, and organic matter is added.

Over time, elements like wind and water will wear away the topsoil, a process called erosion. After the wind blows away healthy soil, rainfall leads to flooding and further breakdown of soil. But human activities like farming also contribute to erosion.

This caused the Dust Bowl in the 1930s. At that time, eroded and over-farmed soil in the central United States blew away in the wind, causing huge dust storms.

Climate change can also lead to more variations in rainfall and droughts, leading to more erosion. Too much rain can wash all the healthy soil away, and droughts make it harder for crops to absorb nutrients from the soil. High temperatures can also harm helpful soil bacteria.

To combat this problem, farmers can plant shrubs to shield their soil from the wind,

grow cover crops (which are plants that are grown on top of profitable crops to help soil health),

and rotate the areas in which livestock graze so different areas of the soil will have time to recover.

Pesticides and Fertilizers

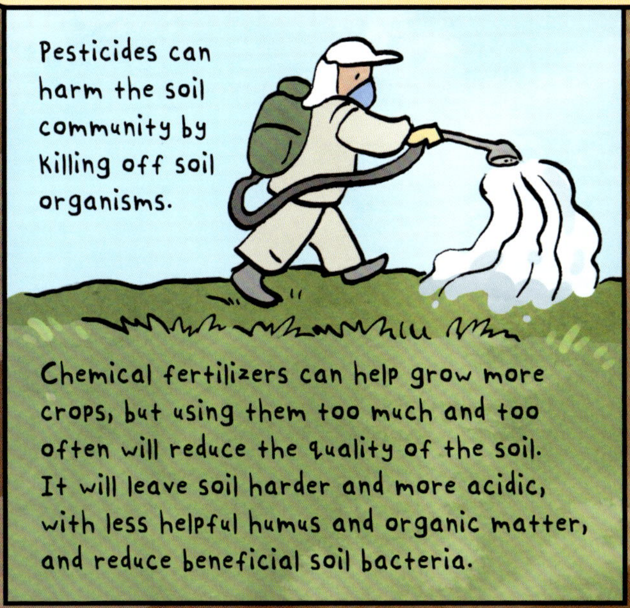

Pesticides can harm the soil community by killing off soil organisms.

Chemical fertilizers can help grow more crops, but using them too much and too often will reduce the quality of the soil. It will leave soil harder and more acidic, with less helpful humus and organic matter, and reduce beneficial soil bacteria.

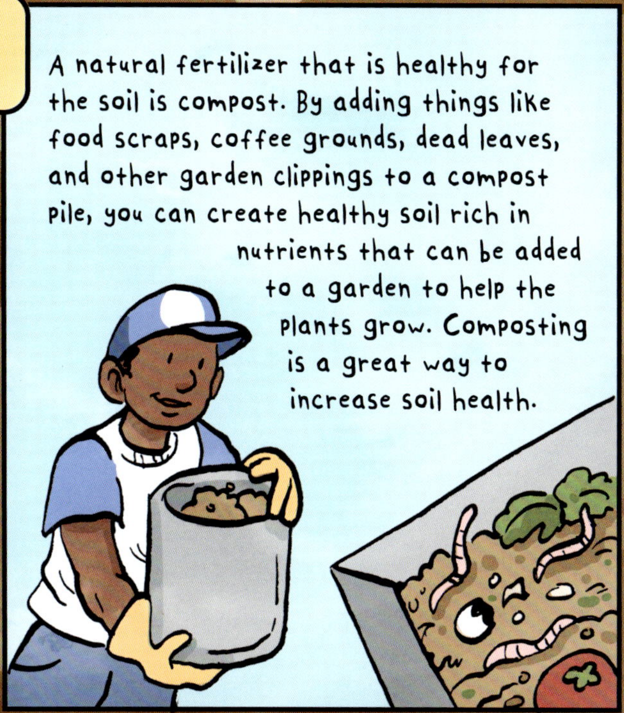

A natural fertilizer that is healthy for the soil is compost. By adding things like food scraps, coffee grounds, dead leaves, and other garden clippings to a compost pile, you can create healthy soil rich in nutrients that can be added to a garden to help the plants grow. Composting is a great way to increase soil health.

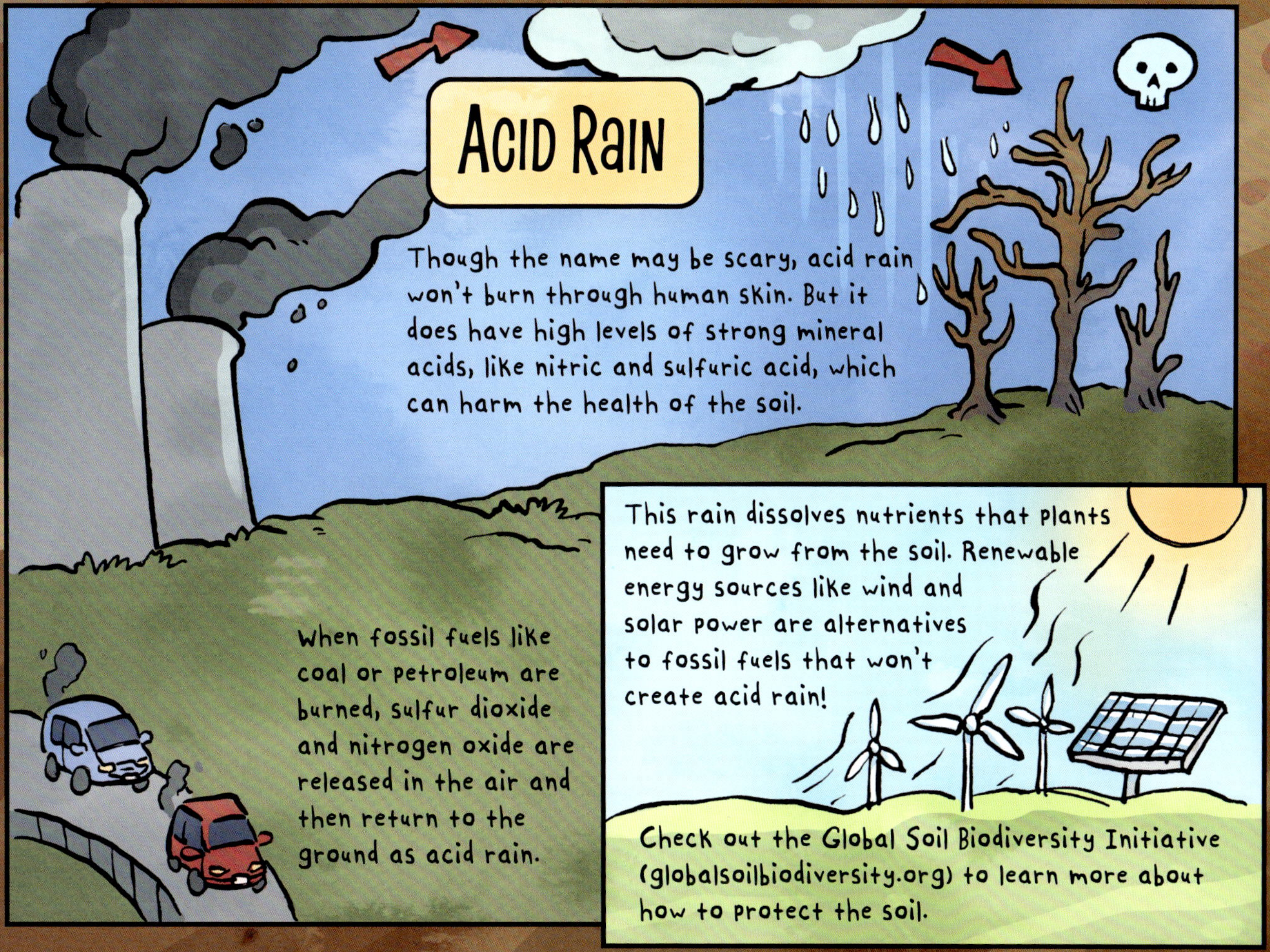

Acid Rain

Though the name may be scary, acid rain won't burn through human skin. But it does have high levels of strong mineral acids, like nitric and sulfuric acid, which can harm the health of the soil.

When fossil fuels like coal or petroleum are burned, sulfur dioxide and nitrogen oxide are released in the air and then return to the ground as acid rain.

This rain dissolves nutrients that plants need to grow from the soil. Renewable energy sources like wind and solar power are alternatives to fossil fuels that won't create acid rain!

Check out the Global Soil Biodiversity Initiative (globalsoilbiodiversity.org) to learn more about how to protect the soil.

INDEX OF SOIL CREATURES

Let's Leave the Leaves!

Instead of raking the leaves when they fall in your yard this fall,
sit back and just leave them! The leaves will provide a safe shelter
for many different critters, and as the leaves break down, they
will feed helpful bacteria to improve the health of the soil.